rewired heart

finding the freedom of a whole new you

by melinda means

author of *Invisible Wounds: Hope While You're Hurting*
co-author of *Mothering from Scratch* and *Unraveled Roots*

Rewired Heart: Finding the Freedom of a Whole New You

Copyright © 2021 by Melinda Means. All rights reserved. No part of this publication may be reproduced, distributed, or transmitted in any form or by any means, including photocopying, recording, or other electronic or mechanical methods, without the prior written permission of the publisher, except in the case of brief quotations embodied in critical reviews and certain other noncommercial uses permitted by copyright law. For permission requests, email the publisher at newthingcreations@gmail.com.

Printed in the United States of America.

First Printing, 2021

Unless otherwise indicated, all Scripture quotations are taken from the Holy Bible, New Living Translation, copyright © 1996, 2004, 2015 by Tyndale House Foundation. Used by permission of Tyndale House Publishers, a Division of Tyndale House Ministries, Carol Stream, Illinois 60188. All rights reserved.

Scripture quotations from The Authorized (King James) Version. Rights in the Authorized Version in the United Kingdom are vested in the Crown. Reproduced by permission of the Crown's patentee, Cambridge University Press.

Scriptures taken from the Holy Bible, New International Version®, NIV®. Copyright © 1973, 1978, 1984, 2011 by Biblica, Inc.™ Used by permission of Zondervan. All rights reserved worldwide. www.zondervan.com The "NIV" and "New International Version" are trademarks registered in the United States Patent and Trademark Office by Biblica, Inc.™

Scripture taken from the New Century Version®. Copyright © 2005 by Thomas Nelson. Used by permission. All rights reserved.

ISBN 978-0-9978470-2-4

Cover and interior design by Melinda Means.
Cover and interior heart images by jozsef - Atilla Nagy © 123RF.com.
Interior prescription form image by jes2ufoto © 123RF.com.

*To every broken, hurting woman hungry for
wholeness who is brave enough to make choices
to find and know the Healer.*

contents

Hello, Beautiful New Friend	vi
Study Format & Leader Helps	viii
Meet a Whole New Me	1
Week 1: *Heart Gone Haywire*	9
Week 2: *Questions of the Heart*	31
Week 3: *Seen by the Doctor*	59
Week 4: *Do You Want to Get Well?*	83
The Prescription: REST	104
Week 5: *Reduce Distractions*	109
Week 6: *Eat from the Feast of God's Word*	119
Week 7: *Surrender to His Love*	139
Week 8: *Trust Him Step by Step*	151
Week 9: *Renewal Comes through Repetition*	161
Resources	176
About the Author	178
Acknowledgements	179
Notes	181

hello *beautiful* new friend,

It is so wonderful to be able to meet with you here in these pages. Whatever hurt and brokenness you are experiencing as you start this journey, know this: Healing is possible. I am living proof.

God gave me the inspiration, truths, and principles for this study in 2017. I wanted to write it then, but I knew I needed time to let His truths sink deeply into my mind and heart. I wrote a good portion of it in 2019 and then felt God lead me to set it aside as He performed more healing in me. I picked it up again in early 2020 — just before the world was plunged into a pandemic. God's timing is always perfect. I can't remember a period in my lifetime where the need for mind, heart, and body healing is so apparent.

I have a fair amount of personal experience with a tortured mind, wounded heart, and sickly body. I have also had a front row seat as I've watched precious loved ones battle depression, anxiety, bipolar disorder, ADHD, and other mental, emotional, and physical conditions.

So often we try to treat the conditions and symptoms of the mind, heart, and body without properly understanding and applying the Treatment — Jesus. I know I did for most of my life. But my lifelong battle with anxiety, woundedness, and physical issues didn't begin to shift until I began to see the Treatment more clearly. Jesus truly is the Great Physician. His love is the Treatment that continually heals my hurts and renews my mind. I can say that, not just because I read it in the Bible, but because I experience it daily.

As I've gone to the Doctor time and time again, He's shown me that while healing is possible, it isn't passive. It is our *choice* whether we truly want to get well. It's not about *earning* our healing. It's about *receiving* the healing that He readily offers. He lovingly invites us to get well, but He doesn't force us.

Healing is going to look differently for each of us because we are each so unique. Clearly, not everyone experiences physical healing this side of heaven, for reasons I don't always understand. But this is what I do know: It's impossible to get closer to the Healer without experiencing some level of healing.

Each of us needs to know His love and care for us in our *hearts*, not just our heads. I invite you to get to know the Doctor better — not just information *about* Him, but Who He *truly* is. As His love captures your heart, you'll find the freedom of a whole new you.

Much Love,

Melinda

study format

Chapter Overview. Each chapter begins with a two-to-three page overview that gives readers a glimpse of what we will be studying that week.

Read & Reflect. In this section, we will dive into the chapter's topic more deeply through Scripture and author insights. Readers are encouraged to reflect on the material and questions thoughtfully, with an open mind and heart, asking God to show them more of Who He is. Each "Read & Reflect" section ends with a "Your Heart Rewired" section that encourages the reader to reflect on and commit to memory those statements about God that resonated with them. A new heart begins with a renewed mind.

A Heart Rewired. In Chapters 1-4, each "Read & Reflect" section is followed by a study of a character of the Bible whose heart was rewired by their encounter with Jesus.

The Prescription: REST. Chapters 5-8 focus on four biblical principles that when applied consistently, bring us into deeper relationship with God.

leader helps

This study was designed to be used individually or in a group setting. If you are leading a group through *Rewired Heart*, I first of all want to say, *thank you*. I know very well the sacrifice and time investment you are making. I want to provide you with guidance and helpful leader resources to enhance your experience and confidence as you lead this study.

You'll find these free resources and more available on my website by visiting **http://newthingcreations.com/rewired-heart-leader-helps**.

- Leader Guide

- Group Guidelines

- Group Session Videos

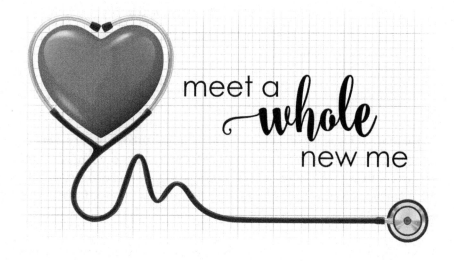

> *. . . anyone who belongs to Christ has become a new person. The old life is gone, a new life has begun!*
> **(2 Corinthians 5:17)**

For most of my adult life, I led a desperate, fractured existence. I experienced bursts of spiritual renewal and energy, but I could never seem to sustain them. Years of health and family struggles had taken their toll. Ultimately, I felt like the life had slowly drained out of me. I felt trapped and broken.

While I looked perfectly healthy, my body was often racked with pain from a host of autoimmune disorders. My mind and heart had suffered blows that I increasingly did not have the power to bounce back from. You see, virtually nothing in my life had turned out like I had once imagined and dreamed. Nothing was like I thought it would be. Too many disappointments over the years had led me to curb my expectations, for my own protection. I had failed or been let down too many times.

In 2015, during a very difficult stretch in my health journey, God brought me to a point where I realized He is my only hope. Doctors, supplements, and diets did not have that power. I couldn't control my health. I couldn't control the people around me. I couldn't control my circumstances. And believe me, I'd tried. But finally, I was just too weary to try anymore. My desperation led me to a life-changing realization: Jesus, *You* are my only hope.

And I believe He smiled and said, "Finally, Child. Now I have something to work with."

Jesus began to open my eyes to my Father's sweetness and goodness to me even in the midst of my pain. Mercifully, the first cracks began to form in the legalistic, demanding view of God that I'd grown up with. I was starting to believe that He wasn't punishing me. He was truly compassionate. I still didn't understand why He allowed me to suffer, but I was beginning to believe He is good.

I began to let go of what I thought my life should look like in ministry, family, parenting, marriage, and health. I let go of trying to meet others' expectations. Trying to figure it all out and make things happen my way had overwhelmed me and left me feeling trapped and drained. Jesus began to show me how to choose to trust and follow Him step by step. It felt good. I was beginning to feel free. But I unconsciously still clung tightly to my incredibly unhealthy and poisoned view of God.

the start of a whole new life

While the first sparks of a whole new life had started in 2015, God began to do something new again in early 2017. Yet another stretch of physical and emotional brokenness had brought me to my knees. This time, God wanted to meet me there to dismantle what remained of the barrier of fear and legalism that stood between us. I believed Jesus loved me. He had always seemed approachable. But although I had recognized glimpses of God the Father's love, I struggled to believe that He could ever truly be pleased with me. My belief in God's goodness was only head knowledge. It hadn't made its way to my heart.

That spring, God began to reveal Himself to me in a way I had never experienced Him before. It was as if Jesus took a step back and said to me, "I want you to meet My Father. And He's not Who you think He is. I'm stepping back so you can see Him more clearly." As my eyes were opened, I felt a level of love I didn't know existed. I said, "Oh, my goodness! If this is Who You really are, God, I want more of this. I want more of YOU." Slowly, He began to lead me away from media, politics, Facebook, and so many other things that were clogging my heart and mind. Even though my circumstances hadn't changed, I felt a level of joy, peace, and freedom that I had never experienced before. I told my husband one day, "I am having fun in my relationship with God for the first time. *Ever.*" I didn't think that was allowed.

Shortly after that, GOD brought this thought to me: *You're having so much joy because you are finally serving the real God. You have been serving the false god of performance. The closer you get to the real Me, the more you are experiencing joy, grace, love, peace, freedom. I don't just give you those things. I AM those things.*

from death to life

A few days later, He led me to a journal that my great-aunt had written to memorialize the life of her sister — my grandmother — who died at the age of 26. My mother told me that her death followed a surgery meant to fix damage caused by multiple abortions. It was painful for my mom to discuss her mother's death and she never went into a lot of detail. Few, even within the family, knew about my grandmother's abortions. As I read this journal — one I had found years ago and stuck in a box unread — I discovered that my grandmother underwent surgery "to correct the bladder problem that had bothered her since childbirth." Days later, an embolism went to her heart and killed her. I can't know for sure, but I believe my aunt wrote "childbirth," since no one spoke of the abortions.

Regardless, those words "bladder problem that had bothered her since childbirth" jumped off the page to me in neon. That was *exactly* how my physical wilderness started. My first physical symptoms of sickness started in the hospital shortly after the birth of my first child. In fact, I found out many years later that the trauma of childbirth flipped a genetic switch in my body that caused a host of autoimmune disorders, starting with a tormenting and painful bladder condition called interstitial cystitis.

As I read that journal, God clearly said to my heart, "Satan has been attacking life in your family for generations. What he used to destroy your grandmother, I am using to draw you to Me and heal you. You know the real Me now. You pray in the power of the real God to break this generational bondage."

I prayed out loud right then and there that God would break the bondage that had held my family hostage for so long. He opened my eyes to the long history of Satan's attack on life in the women in my family — infertility, abortions, endometriosis, near miscarriages, ovarian cancer, early hysterectomies. God was breaking it! I woke up the next morning and the first thing in my head, before I was fully awake, was the thought, *You are a new creation*.

a life-changing realization

On my way to church that morning, I thought about how I had been feeling better over the last couple of months. My migraines, bladder pain, and energy levels had greatly improved. My need for thyroid medication was slowly decreasing. But for the first time, *I got it*. He was healing me physically, as well as spiritually. *I am a new creation!* I pulled into the church parking lot and wanted to tell someone as soon as possible. Someone who would truly "get" the significance of this amazing realization I had just made.

This feeling of exuberance was a stark contrast to four years before, when I went to church one Sunday in a deep state of despair and brokenness. Back then, few people knew I struggled so much physically. That morning, I ran into Sandy, a sweet woman I hadn't seen in months. She was wearing a halo brace after a recent difficult spinal surgery. God sent this "angel" with a halo to ask me how I was doing. I broke down, and for the first time, I shared my struggle to someone outside my close family and friends. Amazingly, she told me that she had the same rare autoimmune condition I had (that most people have never heard of) and that God healed her. She then said with absolute conviction: "I believe He is going to heal you, too."

So fast forward to four years later. Who was the first person I ran into the day I realized I was being made whole? That's right: *Sandy*. The first person who spoke healing over me was the first person God put in my path to share that I was being healed. She hugged me and said, "You look young and beautiful and *new*." Yep. Full of new life.

the Life that was always there

A few moments after talking with Sandy, I walked into the church service. It was communion Sunday. *I hadn't taken communion in three years.* My diet had become so restrictive over the years that I was afraid to eat anything that might trigger pain symptoms. That morning, with tears running down my cheeks, I heard the Holy Spirit say, *This won't hurt you. This is what healed you.*

He had already given me my healing by access to Him through the death of His Son. I had looked for it in performance, ministry, family, doctors, and supplements. These are all good things, but they were not meant to be my saviors. It wasn't that God didn't allow those things to heal me. They *couldn't.* He loved me enough to wait until I was ready to see the real Him. Then, He spoke to me sweetly in my wilderness (see Hosea 2:14), gave me eyes to see and won my heart.

As I began to seek Him more and more, He began to lead me out of my wilderness of spiritual and physical bondage. He was not withholding it before; His deliverance was there all along. I just didn't see it. As I sought His direction and leading, He led me to the real Him and provided me with people and tools to help me unlock and address the root causes of my physical and emotional ailments.

I don't claim to understand all the mysteries of healing. I think the journey often looks differently for each of us because we are each so unique. God's ways with us are tailor-made to how He designed us. I don't pretend to know all the answers. But here's what I do know: I was sick and broken. *Now I am healing.* I felt in bondage. *Now I feel free.* You cannot get closer to the Healer without experiencing some level of healing. God designed our mind, heart, and body to be intertwined. One cannot be affected without impacting the other two. I can only share my experience, but as God began to heal my mind and heart, it led to gradual, but unmistakable physical healing as well.

My healing is an ongoing process, a journey toward wholeness that I am still on, but I am *not* who I was. He is remaking me. He continues to detox me physically, emotionally, and spiritually. He is peeling layers of toxicity from my mind, body, and heart. He gently brings old wounds and faulty belief systems to the surface so He can reveal them and heal them. My joy and love for God continues to increase exponentially. Recently, I had my blood work done. All my levels were within normal range — without medication — for the first time in 15 years! Yes, I still have days when I'm in physical pain — when symptoms seem a lot more real than the healing I've experienced. I still sometimes struggle with old mindsets and wounds. But I am *not* who I was. And I'm not who I *will* be, as I continue to walk with the Healer.

it's time to meet the Doctor

Freedom doesn't just happen to us. It is a condition we have to claim every moment. Everyday. No matter how we feel. No matter what our circumstances tell us. Walking it out is sometimes excruciatingly difficult. It's painful when toxins — both spiritual and physical — leave our bodies, minds, and hearts. However, God has assured me that any pain now is an indication of my healing, not my sickness. They are life pangs, not death pangs. God doesn't just give life. He *is* Life. It took time for me to truly find Him, but the healing and wholeness I'd always wanted had been there all along. He was nothing like I thought He would be, and better than anything I had ever imagined.

When I discovered Who He really is, I began to discover a whole new me. I'm embracing the freedom of living a whole new life. I'm no longer walking *wounded*. I'm walking *healing*.

But I'm just the patient. Get to know my Doctor — really know Him — and that will change everything. Consider *Rewired Heart* my five-star review for the Great Physician.

You may think, *The Great Physician? You mean God? I already know Him. I've known Him all my life.* I thought so, too. But often we've just "heard" about the Doctor. Or we know *facts* about Him. So many times, often well-meaning people — parents, teachers, and others — give us information that is incredibly flawed. We've relied on others' "reviews" or we've equated our life experience with Who God is. We suffer and so we believe

God isn't good or loving. In some cases, we don't need to know *more* information about God as much as we need what we already know to become deeply embedded in our hearts. Wherever we find ourselves, we all need to experience the love of God more deeply. We need the Doctor to rewire our minds and reset our hearts.

His love changes *everything*.

> *Hearts are broken through disappointment. Hearts are broken by bereavement. Hearts are broken in ten thousand ways, for this is a heart-breaking world, and Christ is good at healing all manner of heart-breaks.*
>
> ~ **Charles Spurgeon** [1]

One of the sweetest blessings in my life is my friend Ann. God has used her in my journey in more ways that I can count. As I write this, Ann is a (very young) 81 years old. Many years may separate us in age, but right from the beginning, our hearts connected in a way that transcends generations.

A while back, Ann began to have heart problems. The first symptoms were fuzzy thinking and loss of energy. After a frightening trip to the hospital, the doctor ordered some tests and discovered that Ann's heart was beating out of rhythm. And when the heart doesn't beat correctly, it throws off the entire body.

After medication proved ineffective, she had a cardiac ablation procedure. Using this technique, the cardiologist freezes or "scars" abnormal heart tissue in an effort to correct the rhythm. The procedure worked for a short time, but then the problem returned.

Finally, the doctor told her the best remedy would be to cardiovert her heart. During cardioversion, a cardiologist uses charged paddles to briefly stop the heart and reset it to its proper rhythm so that it can beat the way it was designed to beat. It worked. Her heart is now in rhythm. She almost immediately experienced a renewed level of energy and mental clarity.

Just this morning, Ann sent me this text: "Tonight was the first time to go over 5,000 steps [with her Fitbit®]. I (had) set 5,000 as my new goal. Lost another five pounds. Total of 30 pounds lost . . . I walk with my head held high. I actually enjoy walking. Do you believe it? Yay, God." When our hearts beat as God designed, we enjoy the walk, friends. We begin to drop the weight that burdens us and holds us back. We can walk with our heads held high. We walk *free*.

We all have a heart problem that only God can fix. Our hearts, although imperfect, start out soft and open to our Creator. But something happens along our journey. Our hearts become clogged. They gradually become hard, jaded, and dysfunctional due to sin, disappointment, lies, pain, and woundedness. We build up walls to protect ourselves from further pain and disappointment. And our hearts begin to beat more and more out of rhythm with our Creator.

We instinctively know that something is wrong, but we're not sure how to fix it. We can't think straight. We feel burdened and tired. We grasp at many things to restart our hearts. At times, we get spiritually recharged and renewed, but then life and struggles crowd in, and we find our hearts falling back into old, abnormal rhythms of self-sufficiency, self-protection, and control.

What we need is the Ultimate Cardiologist. We need the One who designed our heart and knows it better than anyone. He knows exactly where the blockages are and what is preventing it from beating in tune with His.

We so often try to diagnose and treat our own heart problems. It's absurd when you think about it. We trust that a human cardiologist knows our hearts better than we do, yet we're often reluctant to trust the One who *created* our hearts. When we ask for a human heart doctor's help, he doesn't tell us to go to medical school and become a cardiologist. Of course not. He or she conducts tests to reveal the problem and then provides simple guidelines for us to follow.

Simple, but not always easy.

God doesn't expect us to diagnose our own heart problems either, friends. As we seek Him, He reveals those areas that we are often not even aware are diseased or damaged. He tailors His treatment plan to our very specific needs. We don't have to fix. We just to have to follow.

Simple, but not always easy.

Yet He gives us this beautiful, reassuring promise for our healing journey:

> For I hold you by your right hand — I, the Lord your God. And I say to you, 'Don't be afraid. I am here to help you.' (**Is. 41:13**)

As we begin this journey together, will you pray this prayer with me?

Lord, cardiovert my heart. Reset it, so it can work as You designed it to work. Please help my heart to beat in rhythm with Yours. Amen.

read and reflect

Several years ago, I lost my precious father following a long battle with congestive heart failure. The last couple of years of his life involved repeated hospitalizations and slow, but steady, decline. He lived several hours from me, near my sister, but I made trips to see him as often as possible. A few weeks before his death, I went to be with him, realizing it was possibly for the last time.

One day while I was there, he was having a particularly bad day. He was on full mask oxygen and still struggling to breathe. He was mostly incoherent and nothing he said all day really made much sense. Then suddenly, as I was sitting by his bed, he called my name with intense clarity and urgency: "Melinda, Melinda, come here." As I moved closer, he grabbed my hand, looked into my eyes with a tenderness and intensity that I can't describe and so clearly said these words: "I love you. I want you to know that. No matter which way things go, I want you to know how much I love you."

In essence, *that* is the message of your heavenly Father. More than anything in the world, He wants you to know *He loves you*. That no matter what happens, no matter how things go in your life, no matter how bad things look, He LOVES you. *You.* Not just in a collective "God loves the world" kind of way. No, He wants you to know that He loves *you*, individually. *Let that sink in.* The God of the universe loves *you* personally and passionately — more than you can possibly wrap your head around.

He doesn't just want that message in your *head*. He wants that message so embedded in your *heart* that you never question it. Because love is the key. Love changes everything. When we view God's activity in our lives from the lens of love, it changes how we view the past, the present, and the future. It changes how we view suffering and uncertainty. Trust, love, surrender, service . . . all those things begin to flow more naturally as we begin to see and experience God's infinite and all-consuming love for us. No matter which way things go, my friend, *He loves you*. We can always trust His heart.

God didn't just intend for His love to give us *eternal* life with Him forever. He also intended His love to give us *abundant* life right now. Peace. Joy. Freedom. Rest. *Right here. Right now.* Not just survival. Or quiet servitude. Joyful, abundant life.

> My purpose is to give them a rich and satisfying life. (**Jn. 10:10**)

love clouded by lies

Any good patient-doctor relationship includes a thorough review of history. It's important that both parties agree on the basic facts. We need to know that our doctor is trustworthy. It establishes a firm, accurate foundation for a healthy and lasting bond going forward. So if what we're about to explore in this chapter is review for you, bear with me: It's very easy for us to forget or misunderstand key information, even if we've heard it our entire lives.

> *As far as the root facts, the fundamental doctrines, the primary truths of the Scripture, we must from day to day insist upon them. We must never say of them, 'Everybody knows them'; for alas! everybody forgets them.* ~ **Charles Spurgeon** [2]

I know this from firsthand experience. For most of my life, I knew *about* God, but I didn't really *know* Him. I *thought* I did. But I couldn't comprehend God's love for me.

I was just four years old when I prayed and told Jesus I knew I needed a Savior. I told Him I accepted His death on the cross as payment for my sins and asked Him to come into my heart. Even though I was a very little girl, I distinctly remember saying that prayer right after my sweet and well-meaning mother asked me, "You don't want to go to hell, do you?"

I know my mom's heart. She loved me and wanted me to know God. I will forever be grateful to her for that. Her intentions were pure and good. And her question motivated me to say the prayer. But it's impossible to feel secure in a fear-based relationship. So I immediately put a wall up around my heart to protect it from this angry God.

As I grew up, my view of God continued to be tainted by fear and obligation. As I began to experience heartbreaking pain and struggles in my life, it only reinforced my view of a vengeful God who was more interested in punishing me than loving me. How could I possibly go to God for comfort when I believed He was the Source of my pain?

Whatever the adults in my life intended, my heart embraced these lies: God loves you and accepts you as long as you perform for Him. His stern and disapproving gaze is looking for what you're doing wrong, not what you're doing right. And regardless of what you do, you can never really please Him, but work hard anyway because perhaps you can avoid His wrath.

love vs. obligation

Before the world was created, Satan, our *true* enemy, was once an angel who served God. He was an incredibly beautiful and high-ranking angel, but he grew prideful in his beauty and status. He no longer wanted to serve God. He wanted *to be God*. He was jealous of the glory that God received. He wanted it all for himself. Because of this, God cast Satan out of heaven (see Ezekiel 28:14-17). Demons are fallen angels who, like Satan, also chose to rebel against God. Satan and his demons are hellbent (literally) on doing whatever they can to try to steal God's glory and wound His heart. They know that the surest way to do that is to attack, deceive, and destroy His creation (see 1 Peter 5:8). After all, we are the apple of His eye (see Zech. 2:8; Psalm 17:8).

It all started with Adam and Eve. God wanted them to follow and obey Him because He knew it would bring them happiness. But He gave them a choice. He wanted them to desire relationship with Him out of love, not because they had no other option. Influenced by Satan's deception, Adam and Eve chose to be their own gods, and ate the apple in the Garden of Eden — the only thing God had forbidden them to enjoy. We have been rebelling against our Creator ever since. He created a perfect world with valuable, protective guidelines for us to live by. We rejected His plan and His ways. We've wanted to be our own authority and live life *our* way. Yes, God is loving, but He is also *just*. A God of justice couldn't just overlook our sin and rebellion. A price would have to be paid.

In the Old Testament, men and women regularly offered animal sacrifices as payment for their sins. Jesus came to earth to be the once-and-for-all

Perfect Sacrifice and payment for our sins. On the cross, He took all the punishment and wrath our sin deserved (see 2 Corinthians 5:21). Because God is holy and perfect, He can't look on sin. While Jesus hung on the cross, He was temporarily cut off from an awareness of God's presence. God turned His back on *His only Son* when He died on the cross, so He wouldn't have to turn His back on *you and me*.

We don't have to earn our salvation. Like any gift, we just have to *receive* it. When we admit our own inability to save ourselves from our sin and accept Jesus as our Savior, His sacrifice covers all our sins — past, present, and future. When God looks at us, He doesn't see sin. He sees *Jesus*.

After we've accepted Jesus as Savior, Satan — our enemy — can't steal our salvation. So he tries to systematically attack our stability. He wants to steal the joy that comes from the restored relationship we have with our Creator. He knows that unshakeable stability is anchored in a rock-solid heart knowledge of God's love for us and recognizing that we are fully forgiven and accepted by God. The enemy knows that when our eyes and hearts are opened to the depth of God's love for us, his gig is up. He will still try to deceive and attack us, of course, but his deceptions increasingly lose their power over our minds and hearts. Every adversity we encounter can be answered with this: "I may not understand why this is happening, I may hate my circumstances and my suffering right now, but I *know* how much my Father loves me."

What do the following verses tell us about the character of God?

Ephesians 3:20

He is able to do far more abundantly than we ask or think...

Isaiah 30:18

The Lord waits to be gracious to you ... He exalts Himself to show Mercy to you.

Nehemiah 9:17

You are a God ready to forgive, gracious & merciful, slow to anger and abounding in steadfast love (and did not forsake them.)

Psalm 69:16

... your steadfast love is good, according to your abundant mercy.

When Jesus came and died for our sins on the cross, He showed us what true love and humility looks like. We don't have to depend on our own performance and works to try to earn God's favor. We don't serve Him out of fear and obligation anymore.

Instead of fear of punishment, Jesus' desire is that our love for Him, and gratitude for what He did for us on the cross, will inspire us to serve Him. Instead of overwork, He desires for us to serve Him from an overflow of love and gratitude.

> Then Jesus said, 'Come to me, all of you who are weary and carry heavy burdens, and I will give you rest. Take my yoke upon you. Let me teach you, because I am humble and gentle at heart, and you will find rest for your souls. For my yoke is easy to bear, and the burden I give you is light.' **(Matthew 11:28-30)**

In these verses, Jesus is saying to us that He will give us rest from having to earn our salvation. He paid the price. His sacrifice covers our sins. He then tells us to take His yoke upon us.

Oxen are paired together by a yoke when they are pulling a heavy load. An older, more experienced ox leads the younger, immature ox. The calf simply follows the older ox who bears most of the weight. Jesus is telling us, "You don't have to carry all the weight of your sin and circumstances. I've taken the weight of your sin. As you share with Me and trust Me with you worries and burdens, I will gently help and lead you. I will show you the way. It may not always be easy, but you can rest in knowing you are not alone. I am here with you, every step of the way."

I'll never forget the day it dawned on me that my walk with God wasn't driven by fear anymore. I had just finished a very full week of serving my family and others, but I wasn't burned out. I felt invigorated. In fact, I ended the week with a smile on my face. I spontaneously told God, "It is my *joy* to serve you." My *joy*. Actually, it was *His joy* that I was experiencing. The joy of partnering with a loving God.

heart exposed

Testing is necessary to illuminate what is ailing the heart. Human cardiologists need to run tests because they can't see inside the heart without special equipment. But God is not subject to those limitations.

> The Lord doesn't see things the way you see them. People judge by outward appearance, but the Lord looks at the heart. (**1 Sam. 16:7**)

We tend to think that if people or circumstances in our lives change, we will finally be content. God sees the real problem, though. The one lurking inside of us. I think God gently says, "I want to change *your heart*. I want you to know that no matter what happens, I am here. I won't ever leave you or forsake you. I want you to see how your heart sickness is contributing to the frustration, restlessness, and fear you're feeling. Let Me help you. "

We often assume that God is testing us to see how *we* will handle things, to reveal *to Him* our level of strength and weakness. Guess what? *God already knows that!* God allows testing — often in the form of difficulties and challenges — to reveal *to us* areas of strength and weakness that we may not have known we had. We may find that we are vulnerable in areas that we thought we were strong. Unaddressed weak spots and wounds slowly drain the life out of us. It's only when we realize the depth of our sickness and need for salvation that we begin to be motivated to place our hearts in the hands of the Healer.

Read Hebrews 4:12. According to this verse, what does God use to show us the sickness in our hearts? How have you seen this in your own life?

but will it hurt?

If you're like me, you'd probably prefer to be put under anesthesia for any type of testing. Just wake me up and give me the report! God doesn't work that way. He never promises that His testing and refining won't cause us pain. In fact, quite the opposite.

Take a look at Hebrews 12:11. What do you think Paul means by "discipline"? How is discipline different than punishment?

painful trials meant to bring the fruit of R+

discipline is a training, punishment is a consequence

Write down a specific instance where you have seen God's discipline be beneficial in your life.

Marriage
Mother
Deaths

How did you feel during the time you were going through it?

horrible to almost suicidal from pain

Although it is usually painful, God doesn't reveal anything He doesn't want to heal. No good cardiologist would ever say to you, "Your tests reveal you have some pretty serious blockages. Alrighty then, now you know the problem. Good luck with that!" Or "Snap! I've never seen anything like that before. Not sure what to do about *that*. Oh well, have a nice day!"

God is a precise, all-knowing Surgeon. But surgery is painful. Your whole heart might have to be exposed. Think about open-heart surgery. The chest has to be cracked open and rib spreaders are used to expose the heart. That is the only way the surgeon can access the areas of the heart that need to be repaired. Even once those areas are mended, recovery can be incredibly long and difficult.

In order to place our hearts in God's hands, we have to know, to the depths of our being, that the pain that surgery brings doesn't mean that God *doesn't* love us. It means that He *does*. He wants to heal our hearts of those things that are killing us. He's doing it to bring us life.

head vs. heart

When my kids were growing up, so often I would impart some word of wisdom or advice to them and they'd say in an exasperated tone, "I know, Mom, I know . . ."

But then they wouldn't do what I advised. They wouldn't act on it. Even though it was often pretty darn good advice, deeply rooted in my love for them. Why? Because they didn't *really* know. They knew what I was saying was right. They often knew it in their heads, but not in their hearts. It was intellectual knowledge, but not deep, to-the-core-of-their-being knowledge. They didn't really know it from life experience. They didn't fully understand *in their hearts* how deeply rooted in love my words to them truly were.

> **Action comes from the heart.** We make choices based on what we believe in our hearts, not in our heads.

About five years ago, God began to open my eyes to the truth: He loved me no matter what. I was *beginning* to believe that my lifelong view of Him as an angry "lightning bolt" God just might not be the truth. But I couldn't stop myself from continuing to chase results and outcomes. I didn't trust His love for me yet. It was the only way I knew. But I had run out of energy for performance-based faith. I was desperate for a new way to live. By the beginning of 2017, I was begging GOD to show me. And then, out of the blue one morning, God really *did* hit me with a lightning bolt. *Just not the one I'd envisioned.*

As I opened my Bible— as I had so many mornings before — I suddenly saw Scripture with new eyes. And the God who was revealing Himself to me was beautifully, irresistibly, shockingly *unfamiliar.*

In dramatic fashion, as I read words I'd read many times before, God sifted truth from lies. I felt God's overwhelming, personal love for me in a way that literally took my breath away. After four incredibly life-changing hours that morning, I closed my Bible and thought, "Whatever I just experienced, I want more of *that*. If that's who You really are, God, I want more of YOU."

I prayed the prayer to accept Jesus into my heart when I was just four years old. I grew up in the church and in a Christian home. I went to a Christian college. I'm currently on staff at my church and have been leading Bible studies for more than 20 years. I've written Christian books.

But here's what I discovered: We can have a lifetime of *head* knowledge about God, but not understand in our *hearts* who God truly is. Only recently has the truth in my head been downloaded into my heart. The depth and scope of His loving and overwhelming nature and personal love for me has taken me by complete surprise. As my heart softened, the wall I started building around it when I was just a little girl began to crumble, brick by brick.

more of Him

We live in a society that is geared toward information overload. Despite being constantly bombarded, we are still thirsting for more: more knowledge, more media, more online courses . . . more, more, more. You know what we truly need more of? *God.* More time with Him. More resting at His feet. More love for Him. More heart knowledge of who He *really* is.

That's what *I* needed! I needed *Him*. I needed Him to gently open my eyes to the depth of His overwhelming love for me. The love that was there all along, but I just couldn't see. It has enabled me to view so many tragic, confusing, and painful circumstances in my life through a different lens. Instead of looking back in frustration, grief, and resentment, God began to show me stunning evidence of His love, sweetness, and activity through those dark, difficult times and places. I began to see how they were all being weaved together as part of His plan and purpose for me. They were not random heartbreaks. He didn't *cause* them, but He did *allow* them for a myriad of reasons. I've begun to understand some of the reasons. Some I may not know until I get to heaven. But I do know this: They brought me to a place where I was willing to give up my own way of doing things and let Him lovingly teach me a better way. And I can say with absolute sincerity that seeing Him as I do now was worth all the pain along the way.

your heart rewired

What truths or statements about God's character from this week's lesson do you most need embedded in your heart? **Write them here and meditate on them throughout the week:**

How very much God loves me.

a heart rewired

the woman at the well

God's love has the power to rewire a woman in just one conversation. God knows exactly when and how to open our eyes to more of who He really is. He meets us exactly where we are and lovingly engages us, inviting us to drink from His living water.

John 4 gives an account of a woman from the town of Samaria. She is also often known as "the woman at the well." Let's start with a little background. Historically speaking, for a variety of reasons, Jews and Samaritans generally hated one another. Women, during that time, were also looked down upon — often regarded more as property than as people. For those reasons, it was shocking for Jesus, a Jewish man, to approach this Samaritan woman.

This is a woman who isn't used to being treated with value and respect. The story gives us clues about her reputation — one that isolates her and impacts how she views herself. She has likely been labeled by her choices. **Bear all these facts in mind as you read John 4:1-30.**

Verse 4 says that Jesus "had to go through Samaria." It was not the only route to arrive at his destination. So why did He *have* to go through Samaria? Jesus will always go out of His way to win a hurting heart.

Most often, women would go to the well in groups early in the day, while it was still cool. It was a daily source of community and socializing. By contrast, the Samaritan woman came at noontime alone. Why do you think she would do this? What do you think this suggests about her relationships with other women?

She was avoiding because she was shunned.

Jesus simply engages her in conversation — a simple, but impactful gesture. Why do you think He started by asking her a question?

To draw her out, make her feel seen

Jesus broke all the cultural rules to talk to this woman. What does that tell you about His character and what He values most?

people over culture

What question did she ask Jesus? (v.9)

Jesus answered her question by saying, "If you only knew the gift God has for you and who you are speaking to, you would ask me, and I would give you living water." (v.10)

In essence He's saying, "Oh, sweet woman, if you only knew Who I am, you would know why I'm here. I came here for *you*. If you knew Who I was, you would ask me for the lasting hope I offer you. You can't see Who I really am, but My love is about to help you see Me clearly."

She still doesn't understand. She is seeing through a human lens. God wants her to see through the lens of His love.

Look at verses 16-19. Why do you think Jesus confronted her in this way? What tone do you think He used? Her ultimate response in verses 28-29 may give you some insight.

Before that critical moment, how do you think his approach during their conversation might have opened her heart to His gentle, but piercing words to her?

Jesus knows that when we experience His love, we more readily understand that even His hard words are meant for our good. He never points out our behavior in order to condemn us. He brought up this woman's failed attempts to find fulfillment because He wanted her to realize how truly thirsty she was, how despite the ways she'd tried to fill her heart, she was constantly left feeling like an empty well. Then, He offered Himself as the only lasting and satisfying cure.

What did the woman do after leaving Jesus (v. 28-39)? What does this suggest about how this woman was changed by her encounter with Him?

What was the result of her telling others about how Jesus had changed her mind and heart (v.39-42)?

This woman had likely been ostracized by many in her community for years. Why do you think her neighbors suddenly listened to her and went to see Jesus, too?

Jesus confronted this woman's sin *because He loved her*. He knew the way she was living her life was not in her best interest. He loved her too much to leave her in that condition. God's standards are not because He wants to harm us or keep us in submission out of some twisted need for control. They are for *our good*. Tolerating sin in ourselves and others can seem merciful. But is it *really* merciful if it allows harm?

The love and forgiveness God offers should not inspire us to sin more! Romans 6:1-2 says it this way: "Well then, should we keep on sinning so that God can show us more and more of his wonderful grace? Of course not!" Instead, the incredible sacrifice of a Father Who loved us so deeply that He gave His only Son to pay for our freedom — and a Son Who willingly did so — should inspire overflowing gratitude, love, and service to Him.

Love changes everything.

a new view of God: the key to a whole new heart

> *Your eye is like a lamp that provides light for your body. When your eye is healthy, your whole body is filled with light. But when it is unhealthy, your body is filled with darkness.* (**Luke 11:34**)

Our vision is often faulty. Seeing God clearly — through the lens of His love — is the key to understanding how very significant and valuable we are to Him. It frees us from having to earn our worth. It allows us to *rest*. But it is our CHOICE to open our minds and hearts to Him. If we do, our new view of Him will spur us to ACTION — to live differently and to tell others of this amazing God who loves us completely. Based on the passage we just read, let's summarize how the Samaritan woman gained a new view of God and the impact it had:

> **Vision Clouded by Lies:** This woman is looking to imperfect people and things to satisfy the longing in her heart. She likely thinks that the next man will be the one to bring her lasting love, security, and happiness. But she continues to be disappointed.

Choice: She was curious and open to a different way of thinking about things. She asked questions. She is open to a new way of living her life.

The Lens of Love: She realizes she is not alone. She meets Someone who knows her better than she knows herself. He knows everything about her — everything she's ever done — and He still loves her! Jesus is the lasting fulfillment she's been searching for.

Action: She runs to her town and tells everyone about this incredible Man, Jesus, who she has met — Someone who has met her deepest need.

Result: Many in her town came to know the love of Jesus, too. We are still impacted by her story centuries later.

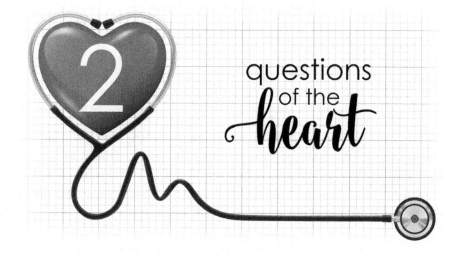

> *Trust in the Lord with all your heart;*
> *do not depend on your*
> *own understanding.*
> **(Proverbs 3:5)**

The question took me by surprise. The year was 2015. I was lying in bed feeling as physically, spiritually, and emotionally broken as I could ever remember. I was weary to the bone from fighting chronic pain and autoimmune disease. Other unrelated, long-standing, heart-wrenching battles had also worn me down.

I was *completely burned out*— and disillusioned with God. Sometime early in my health battles, this lie had taken root in my heart: My earthly father would heal me in an instant if he had the power, and yet my heavenly Father, who has all the power in the world, seems content to allow me to suffer.

Since I viewed God as indifferent to my pain, I set about trying to accomplish my own healing. I tried every diet, doctor, and supplement that seemed to hold any promise. I had just finished a lengthy, painful course of treatment at a clinic two hours from my house.

And I felt worse off than when I started.

I felt numb. Hopeless. I just didn't know how I could continue to live my life in this kind of physical, spiritual, and emotional pain. I had run of energy. I couldn't face more failure. And that's when I heard it. This question came into my mind out of nowhere. I immediately knew it was God: **"Do you trust Me?"**

Because I feared God's wrath, I had always had difficulty being honest with Him without experiencing fear and guilt. But that day, I think my desperation caused me to answer honestly and without hesitation: "I don't know," I told Him. "You aren't looking real trustworthy right now."

Instead of the rebuke I expected, He simply made a gentle statement. A statement that stemmed from His nature — the nature that I couldn't see for most of my life. He made a statement that communicated *love*. And this is what He said to my heart: "You can trust the One who died for you."

It sounds so simple. So *obvious*. But for the very first time that simple truth made its way from my head to my heart. Sometimes we can't truly hear His voice until all the other voices have failed us.

It slowly dawned on me, "Yes. Of course. I can trust the One who died for me! I don't understand why God hasn't healed me. But I can trust Someone who loved me enough to die for me."

That moment was a *huge* turning point for me in my journey — a journey I am still on. God is still unraveling the lies I've believed for a lifetime. It was just the first step toward beginning to believe in my heart that God was truly loving and good. I'm still getting to know this God that I have misunderstood for so long. I'm learning how to trust the love of the Father after years of living in fear of His wrath.

Change is almost always a gradual process. A realization may come in an instant. Walking it out can take much longer. God is a God of process. He patiently walks alongside us and shows us a new way to live, a new way of doing things. As we gradually and more deeply internalize His love, He changes and heals our minds and hearts.

The wounds of rejection, shame, and isolation rarely disappear *immediately*. Transformation takes time. But we can be assured that when we come face-to-face with Jesus — in humility, faith, and brokenness — transformation *will* occur. *And it often starts with a question.*

read and reflect

It is natural and discerning to want to know the credentials of the physician we are going to for our care. We are entrusting a very precious commodity to this person: our health and well-being. Can they be trusted? What titles and credentials do they possess? Are they caring? Compassionate? What is their track record? If they answer these questions well, our trust builds. If their answers are disappointing or evasive, we feel insecure.

If God did nothing else but give His only Son to die for us, He would be worthy of our trust. After all, we have no right to that kind of "treatment." Since Adam and Eve, we have been rejecting Him and rebelling against Him, determined to do things our own way. We weren't worthy of the sacrifice that God and Jesus made for our redemption.

And yet, in addition to saving our very souls, God's character and power provides us with endless reasons for Him to be trusted. If you have ever wondered, *Why? Why can I trust Him?* you're not alone. And I have to answer that with Who — with Who God is. Because the more we understand Who God is, the more we are able to trust Him. When we believe He is good, we find it easier to trust that He is working for our good, even when we don't see how He possibly can be. Let's open our hearts to the possibility that we might just be wrong about Who He is. Let's open our minds and hearts to Who God *truly* is.

I think so often we start with the wrong question. We want to know who *we* are. We want to "find ourselves." We say, "God show me who I am," when, in fact, the best question we can start with is "God, will show me Who *You* are?"

> When Jesus came to the region of Caesarea Philippi, he asked his disciples, 'Who do people say that the Son of Man is?' . . . Then he asked them, 'But who do you say I am?' (**Matthew 16:13&15**)

It's the question that the enemy doesn't want us to ask. He wants to keep us so focused on ourselves — our plans, our purposes, our problems — that we don't focus on Who *God* truly is. When we know the incredible love of God — when we truly internalize in our *hearts*, not just our heads, how much He loves us and is intimately involved in every aspect of our lives — then we don't have to ask who we are. The natural result is that we begin to understand our value, our identity, our worth, our purpose. It just naturally follows. More God-awareness leads to more self-awareness. The more we understand about our Creator, the more we understand how and why He made us.

Question#1: Who Are You, God?

We can never fully know God while we are here on earth. However, that doesn't mean that He can't be known to us *more fully* as we open our hearts to Him. Let's focus on a few of His amazing attributes:

He is Creator.

Every parent can remember the moment they first held their child in their arms. Pure love. Absolutely overwhelming love. The parent looks at that precious, vulnerable little life and they'd do anything to protect that child. They want what's best for them. But as the child grows, the parent knows that sometimes what is best for him or her is going to cause pain.

That's just a glimpse of how God feels about you and me. He created us. He delights in us. He sings over us. He loves us enough to allow us to suffer at times, because He knows it's in our long-term best interest. We are the apple of His eye. He knows us better than we know ourselves. Like any good parent, God's heart grieves when we're in pain, even though He knows suffering is necessary in our lives and is ultimately for our good.

Read Genesis 1. What does it say He did to bring things into being?

Verse 27 tells us we are created in God's image. What do you think that means?

Now let's look at Psalm 139:1-18. How do you feel when you read this passage? What does it tell you concerning how God feels about you and me?

Look at Psalm 139:13. Contrast how we're created with how God created everything else in the universe. What does that suggest to you?

Just like each child is so different, even when they have the same parents, we as God's children are each created so uniquely.

Read Ephesians 2:10. What does this verse tell us about our uniqueness and God's purpose for us?

So often we don't like the way God made us. We want to copy someone else's ways of doing things or wish for someone else's circumstances. You know what God has shown me? *Satan* is the father of formulas. He capitalizes on our human craving to want lives that are neat, comfortable, and predictable. Following a formula gives us a sense of safety and control. Satan wants to rob us of our uniqueness. He tries to make us think we need to be like everyone else. Because Satan is not a creator. He is an imitator, a copycat, a destroyer. If he can rob us of our uniqueness, he can diminish how God wants to uniquely use us.

As we begin to understand more of Who God is — His love and power — we begin to see that He is weaving every quality, wound, and circumstance of our lives into His plan and purpose for us. You have a role in God's plan for the world that only you can play. So do I. We only see a pinprick of God's story and plan and try to make sense of it all. But He doesn't ask us to figure it all out. He just asks us to seek Him, follow Him, and trust Him step by step.

He sees everything.

When I was a little girl, I would play with my sister and the neighbor kids in the woods in front of our houses. One day, we got lost. Everything looked the same and we couldn't find our way back. It was winter. As darkness began to fall, so did the temperature. Our fears, however, began to skyrocket. I didn't have mittens, because that's what kids do. They go playing without their mittens. I sat down on a rock by a little, frozen stream in the woods and began to cry. Out of nowhere, a woman came up to me and said, "Do you need some mittens?" She handed me hers. And then she pointed the way for us to get back home. To this day, I'm not convinced she wasn't an angel. Even if she was not, I believe God sent her to me. I may have felt forgotten, but God never loses track of His daughters.

> Can a mother forget the baby at her breast and have no compassion on the child she has borne? Though she may forget, I will not forget you! **(Isaiah 49:15 NIV)**

He knows us more intimately than we know ourselves. Those painful places we don't want anyone else to see? Those hopes, fears, and doubts we don't dare utter? He wants to meet us there.

He is always there.

God is always revealing more of Who He is. We will never *fully* understand God or His plan for our lives. Until we get to heaven we won't completely comprehend the mysteries of God. We won't have all the pieces of the puzzle. But that doesn't mean we cannot know Him more and more fully. He is everywhere. It is His greatest desire for us to be aware of and enjoy His presence. He delights in it!

Over these last few years, as I've made room for God by pulling back from social media, politics, news, and meaningless busyness, He began to overwhelm me with His love. He opened my mind and eyes to His activity in ways that at times made me laugh and at other times blew. my. mind.

I saw GOD. *Everywhere.* I began to ask Him questions. I asked Him to reveal Himself to me. As I began to pay more attention to my surroundings, as crazy as it sounds, God began to answer those questions and communicate His love in unexpected ways, through ordinary everyday things, like road signs, bumper stickers, and television shows. We began to develop a constant communication, a personal language between Him and me.

Here's what I realized: We often say, "Lord, show Yourself to me. Reveal yourself to me." And I think He sadly shakes His head and says, "I am. I am everywhere. I am all around you. The problem isn't Me revealing myself. Begin to remove the distractions and you'll see Me. You'll begin to hear my voice deep in your spirit. I promise."

As I began to see the real God — a loving Father — I began to experience love, joy, peace, and freedom that I didn't even know *existed*.

When did God last surprise you with something He said or did that you didn't expect?

He's just like Jesus.

One of the most difficult concepts to understand about Christianity is the Trinity. In fact, it's impossible to fully grasp. The Trinity is the foundational truth that there is one God in three Persons: God the Father, Jesus the Son, and the Holy Spirit. Each Person of the Trinity is completely separate, but they are all fully God and have the exact same nature and purpose. Each Person in the Trinity is distinct, but never acts independently of the others. God the Father is the initiator of Creation and salvation (Gen. 1:1; John 3:16); Jesus the Son implements the plans of the Father (John 5:19; John 3:16) and the Holy Spirit lives inside of us when we accept Jesus as Savior. He is our Counselor, Guide, and Comforter (John 14:16-17; 26). He convicts of us sin and teaches us and reminds us of truth (John 16:8).

As I said earlier, the picture of God that I grew up with was as a vengeful and demanding Deity. I wasn't sure I wanted to be known by that kind of God. He seemed scary. I always saw *Jesus* as the gentle, kind Member of the Trinity. Jesus always seemed far more approachable than God. In fact, I now realize that I viewed God as "bad cop," Jesus as "good cop" and the Holy Spirit as Switzerland. He was the "neutral" party that kept God from being too hard on me and Jesus from enabling me too much.

Why does Jesus seem more approachable than God for people like me (and maybe for you, too)?

Read these Scripture verses and passages that give us examples of Jesus' character and nature: Matthew 9:36; John 13:1-17; John 8:1-11; Luke 23:34; John 5:1-9. What characteristics did Jesus display when He was walking here on earth?

What other verses or stories from the Bible come to mind that reflect Jesus' heart?

The disciples were confused about Who God was, too. **Read John 5:19-47 and John 8:19, 25-29.** Jesus gives His disciples great insight about God the Father. What do we learn about God through these verses? Be as detailed as you can.

Jesus could not have been clearer when He spoke to the Pharisees and to His disciples. Nearly every time they asked Him, "Who are You?", He had the same answer: "Anyone who has seen me has seen the Father!" (John 14:9) How could they not get it, *right*?

Well, *gulp*. I read those passages since I was a little girl and I didn't get it either. My childhood view of a vengeful God clouded everything. I couldn't see that Jesus is an exact representation of God the Father. They are separate, but with the *exact same nature*. I couldn't truly experience God's love for me for all those years because I didn't *expect* it. Instead I expected His judgment and disapproval.

When I began to open my heart and mind to the possibility that I might be wrong about Who God is, He blew me away with His love. It was always there, but I could finally see it! When the Bible speaks of "fearing" God, *I did*! Boy, did I. But my idea of what "fearing God" meant was greatly flawed. It negatively impacted my ability to let down my guard and build open and authentic relationship with Him. What I've come to realize is that fearing God means viewing and approaching Him with great awe and respect, to recognizing and honoring His infinite wisdom and power.

He wants to be known by us. In fact, God wants to be seen as He truly is so badly that He sent His only Son here to walk the earth so we could see His love and character in the flesh. Jesus *died* so we could be free from fear of God's punishment. We just have to open our hearts and clear our minds.

Question#2: Are You going to disappoint me?

I have been under the care of countless doctors over the years. I've also been to many doctors to obtain care for my son, Micah, who was diagnosed with cystic fibrosis (CF) as a baby and CF-related diabetes at age 14. Some of the physicians I've visited — particularly those who have cared for Micah — have been highly invested, wise and attentive, even when they were unable to provide me with the answers or relief I craved. But other physicians I encountered were cold and detached and, quite frankly, left me worse off than when I started. Because of those bad experiences, I grew cynical and distrusting of the medical community. Please understand. This is not an indictment of all doctors. Every profession has good and bad practitioners. Even the best doctors make mistakes. And physicians are certainly not the only people who have hurt and disappointed me in my life. *I've* also often been guilty of letting others down and causing them pain. We're all flawed humans.

But what I've realized recently is that over the years, my woundedness has led me to keep my hopes and expectations small. I didn't want to hope too much and be disappointed again. The pain was just too great. God gives many promises in the Bible. They have sometimes seemed too be good to be true. I've been afraid to believe them. My childhood view of God as demanding and vengeful —coupled with disappointments and experiences with people —colored how I viewed God. I often expected Him to act and react just like people do. Like a human.

God becoming human in our heads causes us to instinctively put up walls in our hearts. It keeps God small. Angry and unapproachable. It prevents us from knowing in our hearts how loving, sweet, holy, wise, just, and powerful God truly is.

Even the best physician views you and me as patients. That doesn't mean they don't care, but the relationship is doctor-patient. By design, there is a clinical, detached nature to it. By contrast, when we accept Jesus as Savior, the Great Physician sees you as *family*. As His precious adopted daughter. You can trust the love of Dr. God. He's not just your Physician. He's your loving Father.

While Jesus walked the earth, He was fully man, but *not* flawed. He retained all of His divine nature. He got hungry. He felt pain. He wept tears. But in all His humanness, He was also fully God. He became human, but without our sin nature. Yes, He had the human mind and the will to *choose* sin, but He didn't have any sin nature in Him that caused Him to do things that were hurtful or vengeful or wrong. There was no sin in Jesus; otherwise, He could not have been the perfect sacrifice for our sins. (2 Cor. 5:21)

Once I began to internalize God's love for me in my heart, not just my head, these are some of ways I'd realized that I had made God human:

I believed He expects something in return.

> For it is by grace you have been saved, through faith — and this is not from yourselves, it is the gift of God — not by works, so that no one can boast. (**Eph. 2:8-9 NIV**)

I had a (now-deceased) family member who appeared to be selfless and giving. However, there were always strings attached. When I would upset or disappoint this person, I would be quickly reminded of all they had done for me. I *owed* them. I was pelted with guilt and shame. *But that's not how God treats us.* When God gave us the gift of His Son Jesus, that's exactly what it was: *a gift of love*. What do you do with a *true* gift? It is simply to be received.

Read Romans 3:19-28. I particularly like the NLT version of this passage. According to verse 19, what is the purpose of the law (the commands and instructions given through Moses in the first five books of the Bible)?

Like Israel, no one can keep the law perfectly. No one can attain God's perfect standard. We owe Him everything, but He never comes to collect the debt. What makes us accepted in God's sight (verses 27-28)?

I believed He expects me to produce results.

For years, I longed for certain outcomes. I did everything I could think of to produce them. And mostly, I fell short. Or the results were short-lived. Or they didn't look like I had hoped. Trying to achieve results overwhelmed me. And I finally realized why I was so weary: Results are not my job.

A loving God only invites us to follow Him. One step at a time. Outcomes are up to Him alone. Such freedom in that! I don't have to produce. I just have to follow!

Circumstances and life may overwhelm us. Sometimes the steps God leads us to take will feel scary and overwhelming. But He promises to empower us every step of the way.

> Don't be afraid, for I am with you. Don't be discouraged, for I am your God. I will strengthen you and help you. I will hold you up with my victorious right hand. (**Is. 41:10**)

Obedience, not producing outcomes, is our job. How does this make you feel? Is it freeing? Scary? In what area(s) of your life do you find yourself trying to produce outcomes?

I believed He loves conditionally.

> For I am convinced that neither death nor life, neither angels nor demons, neither the present nor the future, nor any powers, neither height nor depth, nor anything else in all creation, will be able to separate us from the love of God that is in Christ Jesus our Lord. (**Rom. 8:38-39 NIV**)

People can think the worst of us. They judge us by our mistakes and inadequacies. They define us by our failures. What they think or feel about us can change from day-to-day and moment-to-moment. God, on the other hand, always views us through the lens of love. And we are no more worthy of it on our best days than on our worst!

I feared that He doesn't follow through.

> God is not a man, so he does not lie. He is not human, so he does not change his mind. Has he ever spoken and failed to act? Has he ever promised and not carried it through? (**Num. 23:19**)

People — even those who love us dearly — will always let us down. Often, we've experienced so many disappointments, so many broken promises, that we've been conditioned to expect the worst. We harden our hearts to protect us from more woundedness.

So when God promises us something, we can often be afraid to embrace it. We *want* to believe, but our human experience tells us to put our guard up. Total trust becomes impossible. It makes us afraid to give Him everything.

We worry and wonder where God is in the midst of our suffering and heartbreak. We think God has left us. And here's what I think God says to us: "Other people may have disappointed you and left you. But that's not what *I'm* going to do. You may *feel* alone, but you are *not* alone. You may not understand My ways, but you can trust My heart."

Read Deuteronomy 31:6 and Romans 8:11. What is one way in which you believe God wants you to be bold and trusting that scares you? How do these verses encourage you?

Question#3: Why Do I Suffer?

Back in Week One, I told you about a lie that took root in my heart very early in my chronic pain journey: If my earthly father had the ability to heal my pain, he would do it in a second. And yet my heavenly Father, who has all the power in the universe, allows me to suffer. Over the years, that really messed with my head. It began to challenge my belief that God is truly good. Because if He could turn a deaf ear to my suffering — and the pain of so many others — time and time again, how could He *truly* be compassionate and merciful?

Well-meaning people told me over the years, "You just need to have faith that He's going to heal you." So, *if I'm suffering, it's my fault because I don't have enough faith?* That's a heavy load to bear. And I *did* have faith. I *believed* with all my heart that God could heal me. But that left me back where I started — wondering why a good God refused to heal my pain.

Sometimes I *am* the cause of my own pain. I've chosen at times to do things my way instead of God's way and I've reaped the consequences.

In some cases, suffering can be the result of a spiritual attack. At times, God allows tragedy or suffering in our lives for some reason or reasons that we just can't always grasp. Sometimes our pain is simply the result of living in a broken, fallen world. God gave us the ability to choose, and sometimes people choose to do terrible things that wound others. This isn't how He intended life to be.

From the very beginning of time, Satan has been trying to get us to doubt God's goodness.

Read Genesis 3:1-5. What question did Satan ask Eve in the Garden of Eden? What do you think his motive was in asking her this question? How do you think this led to her eating the apple?

Based on this passage and your own experience, what are some of the ripple effects that result from acting on our fear that God isn't really good?

I don't pretend to understand all the reasons why God allows suffering. I simply don't know. That used to bother me so much. But I'm gradually coming to peace with the unknown — with not having all the answers.

The more I've understood God's deep love for me in my heart, the more I've been able to trust Him with the suffering I don't understand. It doesn't mean I like it. It doesn't mean I don't ask Him for deliverance and at times unleash on Him all my messy questions, frustrations, and emotions. But what I always come back to is this: He loves me. He has shown me that again and again. I don't have the answers to all my questions, but His love assures me I can trust Him.

Although we can't fully know God's plan for allowing suffering in the world, I want to touch on a few Biblical principles that can help us when the enemy challenges our belief in God's goodness, particularly in light of our own personal suffering and the pain in the world around us:

Suffering equips us for our purpose.

The entire story of Joseph is lengthy, but we're going to examine portions of it. **Start by reading Genesis 37.** This chapter tells us that God gave Joseph some incredible dreams. He gave him a glimpse of his future. But then, nearly every single thing that happened after those dreams seemed to indicate Joseph's future was grim. How does God giving Joseph those dreams as a boy reflect his mercy and love for Joseph?

Now read Genesis 39&40. How do you think the difficulties that Joseph suffered prepared him for the plan God had for him — to be a powerful leader who saved up and managed resources so that Egypt and Israel could survive a terrible stretch of famine?

In Genesis 45:4-8 & Genesis 50:19-20 Joseph relates the reason why God had allowed him to suffer such hardship for so many years. If Joseph had known from the beginning God's plan for his suffering, do you think that it would have brought him comfort? Why or why not?

As a boy and teen, Joseph was self-assured and maybe a bit full of himself. His years of suffering humbled him. It gave him compassion for others. He gained valuable skills and a deep relationship and trust in God. By the time he met the Pharaoh, Joseph was a man perfectly equipped for his purpose.

Difficulty doesn't mean God doesn't love me.

If God really loved me, surely He'd heal me. For years, that thought came to me over and over again. Of course, I knew this was false. But yet I couldn't shake it. I thought I didn't deserve to be in pain. Gently, God began to bring this question to my mind: What *do* you deserve? Gulp. Well, I certainly didn't deserve Jesus coming to die for me so I could live in heaven with Him one day. Here is a hard truth, friends — one that we often conveniently forget: Living a "good" life, believing in God is not a "get-out-of-suffering" free card. We don't deserve anything. We aren't entitled to any certain outcome. We deserve death. We deserve nothing.

When God allows pain, He always has a plan to use it for my good and His glory. It doesn't mean He doesn't love me. But honestly, when I've been in seasons of terrible, nearly uninterrupted pain, I have just wanted to be *delivered*. I knew that God has a purpose in my pain — *I didn't really care at that moment*. I knew He was using it to build my character and depth of compassion — *but I just wanted relief.* I saw how He was using my pain to help others — *and, frankly, I wanted be less helpful.* I still sometimes struggle in this way when I'm in physical and emotional pain.

I take comfort in knowing that Jesus struggled too. In the Garden of Gethsemane, hours before He was going to be crucified on the cross, He too asked for simple deliverance:

> ... My Father! If it is possible, let this cup of suffering be taken away from me." But then He followed it with: 'Yet I want your will to be done, not mine.' (**Matthew 26:39**)

It reminds me that it is an act of *my* will — powered by the Holy Spirit — to submit to God's plan, even when it means that I won't see an immediate rescue from my pain. It is a *choice* to believe that the God who sent His only Son to die for us loves us passionately, even though we don't understand why He doesn't always relieve our suffering.

Instead of seeking peace in answers — that may or may not come — we can take comfort in clinging to His promise that He will never leave us or forsake us (Deut. 31:6). Awareness of His presence is both sweet and powerful.

Pain gives birth to beautiful things.

> In the same way, I will not cause pain without allowing something new to be born ... (**Is. 66:9 NCV**)

Just as the pain we experience during childbirth gives way to a beautiful child, God can bring beautiful things from pain. It is sometimes an agonizingly long process. As brutal as it may seem, we often have to experience the pain in order to appreciate the blessing.

Many years ago, I attended a women's conference. I remember woman after woman coming onto the stage sharing testimonies of God's love and power in their lives through incredible pain. Out of nowhere, the thought popped into my head, "That is going to be you someday." I didn't immediately recognize it as God's voice. I remember laughing to myself. *Why would I even think that? Me? What would I possibly have to say?*

Yeah, well . . . The years that followed gave me plenty of material. My life experiences, along with God's mercy and activity, gave birth to a writing and speaking ministry both at my church and outside of it. It gave me an ever-deepening sense of compassion for others in pain and, most importantly, a deeper relationship and dependence on God.

Day by day, He has always given me what I've needed to overcome my pain, my emotions, my doubts. Time after time, He has sweetly given me reminders of His love and assurance of His provision. Do I always understand why God allows pain? *No.* But is the loving God that I've come to know more deeply in the middle of it *really* good? I can say "Yes," without a doubt.

the Father's Love

One day, I found myself crying for no particular reason. It wasn't a sad cry. I actually felt really happy and at peace. I wondered, *Then why am I crying?* And I felt God say to my heart: "I'm overwhelming you with My love. That is the *only* time I will overwhelm you."

You can trust Someone who loves you that much. You can rest knowing that He has your back. You can wait on His timing because you know His pace and purpose for you has been lovingly and uniquely calibrated for your personal design and journey. You can persevere through pain and disappointment because you know He keeps His promises.

How we view God doesn't change who He truly is. *He isn't human.* We just need eyes to see.

When we do, His love will always overwhelm us. In fact, it's what heals us.

your heart rewired

What truths or statements about God's character from this week's lesson do you most need embedded in your heart? **Write them here and meditate on them throughout the week:**

a heart rewired

mary magdalene

God isn't afraid of our questioning. He *welcomes* honest, sincere questions. He wants us to know Who He is. God also asks *us* questions. My relationship with God began to change completely when He asked, "Do you trust Me?" at a critical point in my journey. I had to decide what I really believed. That's what questions often do: They snap us out of our mental fog and well-worn thought patterns and behaviors. They cause us to stop and think about what we're doing, why we're doing it, and what we truly believe. It's why Jesus asked people so many questions when He was here on earth. It's why He still asks us questions today. He knows that realizations we make on our own are much more powerful than simply being given the information. He wants us to know the truth of Who He is in our *hearts*, not just in our heads.

Often, we view life from the cloudy lens of our own wounds and expectations. We can become so overcome by our grief and pain, that we can't see the healing and truth that is right in front of us.

Let's take a look at the story of Mary Magdalene. When she first met Jesus, she was in terrible bondage. Luke 8 tells us that Jesus set her free from several demons that plagued and attacked her. He changed her life and she dedicated it to Him. She traveled with Him from town to town.

> Soon afterward Jesus began a tour of the nearby towns and villages, preaching and announcing the Good News about the Kingdom of God. He took his twelve disciples with him, along with some women who had been cured of evil spirits and diseases. Among them were Mary Magdalene, from whom he had cast out seven demons; (**Luke 8:1-2**)

Now **read John 20:1-18**. Let's set the scene: Jesus has been crucified and laid in the tomb. During that time in history, bodies were prepared for burial with spices and perfumes. Since Jesus died on a Friday, there likely was not time to perform these customary burial rituals before the Jewish Sabbath (Saturday), when no work was to be performed.

Mary Magdelene returns to the tomb very early on Sunday to pay honor to Jesus and give Him a proper burial. But she is surprised by what she finds at the tomb.

What *did* Mary find and what did she immediately assume had happened?

Mary runs to find Peter and John, two of Jesus' closest disciples and tells them what she's found. They quickly discover the empty tomb as well. John believes Jesus is alive. However, they aren't sure what they are supposed to do next, so they go back to their homes.

Mary, on the other hand, returns to the grave. Why do you think she returned? What did she do when she got there (v.11)?

Mary didn't understand what was happening. She was greatly upset. She thought Jesus was the Savior and Messiah that the Old Testament prophets said was coming to earth. Like many others, she likely thought He was going to set up a kingdom on earth. Now He was dead. Along with so many of her hopes. But she didn't let her pain and disappointment keep her from searching for Jesus.

How can you "look for Jesus" when you find yourself overwhelmed by disappointment and questioning His goodness and His ways? In practical terms, what are some ways you can do that?

Two angels speak to Mary, but it seems likely that she doesn't recognize them as angels. Her grief doesn't allow her to see anything clearly. Their presence doesn't seem to calm her at all. In fact, verse 14 says that "she turned to leave." Her entire focus is on finding Jesus.

As she leaves, she "saw someone standing there." Who was it? What is her reaction? (v. 14)

Why don't you think Mary recognized Jesus?

Can you think of a time when Jesus was leading or working in your life and you didn't recognize Him until later? Share it briefly below.

Pain and grief have a way of clouding our minds and vision. We can't see straight. We can't think straight. Mary had traveled with Jesus for years. He had said many times that He was going to die and be raised again after three days. Yet we're not so different from Mary. Grief can also cause us to forget what we know to be true. We hear or read God's Word, but in the heat of the moment, or when we're deep in pain or disappointment, we completely forget what He said. Or we fail to fully understand what His Word means.

He asked her the same question as the angels, "Why are you crying?" but then He asked another question. What did He ask? (v. 15)

Questions of the Heart

As we discussed earlier, powerful questions asked at just the right time can be very effective in helping us to stop and think about what we truly believe. In this case, it laid the groundwork for the next thing Jesus said. Jesus says one word that suddenly causes Mary's eyes to be opened. What did He say to her?

What was the result? (v.16)

It's when God speaks His Word directly, personally, and lovingly to our hearts that our eyes are opened. He applies it at just the time we need it and in such a way that we recognize Him in a new way. If we don't give up, our confusion and frustration with God can often ultimately lead us to a deeper level of clarity and spiritual awakening. We are most likely to see Jesus when we are longing and searching for Him — even when we have seen all our hopes shattered and we feel helpless and confused.

When Mary finally recognizes Jesus' voice, *after much seeking*, her grief is instantly transformed to joy. Sometimes it takes much searching and time with God for Him to break through the mental and emotional barriers between us.

Mary wants to stay in that place with Him. But Jesus gently gives her some instructions. What does He tell her to do? (v. 17)

It is surprising to me that as much as Mary longed to find Jesus, nearly moments after she does, she runs to follow His instructions. Why? I believe she now knows to the depths of her being that Jesus keeps His promises, that He is exactly Who He told her He was. She can't help but share the good news with others. The same happens to every heart that sees God for Who He truly is.

a new view of God: the key to a whole new heart

Your eye is like a lamp that provides light for your body. When your eye is healthy, your whole body is filled with light. But when it is unhealthy, your body is filled with darkness. (**Luke 11:34**)

Recognizing God's loving and powerful presence gives us the courage and hope to keep going when we don't understand God's plan or His ways. It is our CHOICE to seek Him and ask Him to open our eyes to who He is, and our ears to His voice. If we do, our new view of Him will spur us to ACTION — to tell others Who He truly is, too.

Vision Clouded by Lies: Jesus is dead. Her hopes seem dead, too. She has no one and nothing that can comfort her. She's confused. The future looks dark and uncertain.

Choice: Mary pushes past her confusion and pain, continuing to seek Jesus even though it makes no sense to do so from a human standpoint.

The Clear Lens of Love: Jesus is right there beside her. She just didn't recognize Him! He promised her that He would never leave her or forsake her. She just didn't understand. She didn't remember.

Action: She follows His instructions to go and tell His disciples that He is alive. She knows she can leave Jesus, because in her heart she now knows that He will never leave her.

Result: Her grief turns to joy. She gets to share the incredible news and see others' lives changed.

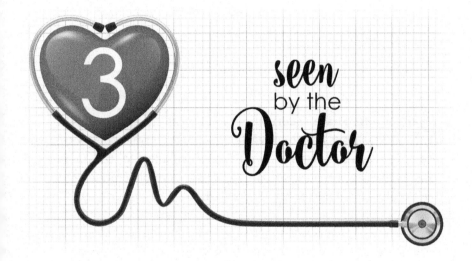

> *But whenever someone turns to the Lord, the veil is taken away.*
> **(2 Cor. 3:16)**

Patients often have a short window of face-to-face time with their doctors. Physicians have to carefully manage their time in order to ensure they can see everyone on their schedules and allow for the unexpected. This reality can result in patient-doctor communication that sometimes feels rushed, incomplete, and disjointed.

I'm so grateful that God doesn't have a limited amount of time to spend with us. He doesn't struggle with how to manage His "patient" load. He doesn't have to maintain a measure of clinical detachment. He longs for us to share with Him every concern and struggle we experience. It's not because He doesn't already know them. He is our Physician and Creator. He knows us better than we know ourselves. But He is also our always loving Father. He longs for deep, intimate, ongoing *relationship* with us. That kind of relationship and trust is only built through sharing our hearts in ongoing and personal communication.

God used a seemingly *insignificant* experience in the middle of the grocery store to make *significant* progress in my understanding of the depth of His love for me.

I was standing in the baking aisle. I began to hear a little girl happily singing, "Happy Birthday to Daddy! Happy Birthday to Daddy!" The little girl's mom was pushing the shopping cart as she bounced in the seat and continued to chatter excitedly about baking the cake and buying presents for her daddy.

I began to smile. Her expressions of love for her father were so cute and sweet. In that tender moment, I heard it. Like a thunderbolt, God spoke to my heart: "Melinda, *that's how I see you*! As my precious, dependent child who I delight in."

God delighted in me? The idea that God *delighted* in me took me by complete surprise. I couldn't quite wrap my mind around it. I was still absorbing that eye-opening truth when God continued to speak to my heart, "Look at the child, Melinda. She is being *led* by the parent, but the parent is not detached. The parent didn't place the child in the seat with her back to her. They are face-to-face! Intimacy! That is what I desire with you. I want to lead you face-to-face. Seek *My face*!"

This was God's design and desire from the beginning of time. In the Garden of Eden, there was no barrier between God and man. Our hearts were in perfect alignment with His. Before Adam and Eve ate the forbidden fruit, they had complete and unhindered intimacy with God. Thankfully, He had a beautiful plan to restore our relationship. His name is Jesus.

read *and* reflect

In an emergency room or hospital, a curtain is almost always around the patient's bed. When the physician comes to examine the patient, he or she pulls back the curtain. They *could* communicate through the curtain, but it certainly wouldn't feel as personal. Pulling back the curtain allows for face-to-face relationship.

In the beginning, there was no curtain. Adam and Eve were completely naked, no curtain, looking straight at the Physician and feeling no shame. **Take a look at Genesis 2:25.** Do you think this verse is only referring to their physical nakedness? What deeper meaning might be implied?

When sin entered the world, a curtain — the barrier of sin — separated us. God in His unfathomable holiness cannot tolerate or look at sin. Sin shattered our ability to experience face-to-face relationship with Him.

Read Genesis 3:1-10. What does verse 10 say? Contrast that with Genesis 2:25. What event caused them to feel naked and ashamed?

Genesis 3:8 says, "When the cool evening breezes were blowing, the man and his wife heard the Lord God walking about in the garden. So they hid from the Lord God among the trees." This is where shame entered the world. It did not exist before. When Adam and Eve sinned, they hid from

God. They sewed fig leaves to cover their shame and nakedness. We've been creating our own "fig leaves" ever since — performance, appearance, comparison, excuses — to feel good about ourselves. What "fig leaves" do you recognize in your own life?

Look up a definition of "shame" and write it here. How do you think shame differs from conviction?

Here's a simple test that always helps me to distinguish shame from conviction: **Conviction energizes. Shame paralyzes.**

When I'm feeling ashamed, I feel defeated and humiliated. It tells me things like, "*You* are such a screw-up. *You* always do this. *You'll* never change." It's an accusing voice that sounds condemning and makes me feel hopeless. If I'm really a screw-up and will never change, what hope is there? I might as well give up.

Conviction feels like a gentle, but firm, awareness of something I have done wrong. It often comes to me as a question. It might sound like, *Why did you do that, Melinda?* or *Is this the best use of your time?* or *Who are you depending on right now — you or Me?* But the tone never sounds gruff or demanding in my head. It's always gentle, but persistent. The Bible calls it a still, small voice. (1 Kings 19:12) Still and small, but somehow it always (eventually!) gets my attention. That loving voice may make me feel uncomfortable, but not condemned. It inspires me to want to change my behavior. It offers grace and correction, giving me hope that change is possible.

Before Jesus died for us, we were in a perpetual condition of shame, naked before God, trying to use our good behavior to cover us. But we always ended up with indecent exposure! We couldn't ever be "good" enough to fully clothe ourselves. We couldn't ever meet God's holy standard. It's sort of like that feeling we get when we're wearing that thin little gown in the hospital or doctor's office and are struggling to keep the strings tied and our bare butts from peeking out.

Jesus uses questions as a teaching technique to promote understanding and healing. Satan uses questions to create doubt and confusion The first recorded words out of Satan's mouth in the Bible are recorded in Genesis 3:1: "The serpent was the shrewdest of all the wild animals the Lord God had made. One day he asked the woman, 'Did God really say you must not eat the fruit from any of the trees in the garden?'" What was the purpose of Satan's question?

What do you think Adam and Eve's perception of God was prior to their decision to rebel? How did Satan's question change that?

Satan used to routinely bring this accusation to my mind: *Do you really think things will ever change? You haven't made any progress at all.* Over and over again, he pelted me with this lie. It made me incredibly discouraged. It zapped me of my energy and resolve.

Eventually, I began to answer him like this, "I *have* made progress! I am *not* who I used to be! He who began a good work in me will complete it. (Phil 1:6)" I began to say those words over and over again whenever Satan whispered to my mind: *Do you really think things will ever change?* And guess what? **He doesn't ask me that question anymore.** As I've repeated truth, it has transformed my mind and thinking in that area! He knows it's useless to try to convince me otherwise. He pelts me with different questions, of course, but I know, as I repeat God's Word, one-by-one the truth will eventually neutralize those questions as well. God's resources are limitless. The enemy's resources are not. He's not going to continue to engage in a losing tactic.

We need to be aware of the source of the questions and statements that come into our minds. Questions from God are life-giving. When Satan is the source, they are designed to create distance between us and God. It's a tactic he's been using since he discovered how beautifully it worked with Eve.

What questions or statements come to your mind most often that you can clearly identify are from the enemy? Look up a Scripture that you can use to answer each question with truth.

What did you learn from Genesis 3:1-10 that might help you to distinguish between positive and Spirit-inspired questions and Satan-inspired questions?

The curtain between us

In Exodus, God used Moses to lead the Israelites out of slavery in Egypt. He told them He was going to lead them from a land of slavery to a land of freedom in Canaan, also known as the Promised Land. God gave Israel His standards and rules through Moses. The Law of Moses includes the Ten Commandments and the rules and regulations outlined by God in the first five books of the Bible. These standards could not be kept perfectly. Israel failed to do so time and time again. A price had to be paid for that sin and rebellion. They didn't yet have continual access to God's presence that was made available through Jesus' death and resurrection. At that time, to meet with God, Israelites had to make themselves "clean" through sacrifice and prayer. In addition, ongoing sacrifices were made at appointed times.

Beginning in Exodus 25:8, continuing through Exodus 26, God instructed the Israelites to construct a portable tabernacle while they traveled in the wilderness from Egypt to the Promised Land. Moses, Aaron, and the priests went to the tabernacle to worship and meet with God to offer animal sacrifices for the people's sins. God gives very specific instructions for building this tabernacle. The innermost room in the tabernacle was called the Holy of Holies. A veil separated this room from the rest of the tabernacle. Only one high priest was allowed to enter the Holy of Holies once a year. This was known as the Day of Atonement, when the priest offered a sacrifice for his own sins and all the sins of the nation of Israel.

Before the high priest could enter the Holy of Holies, he was required to wash himself, put on special clothing, and bring burning incense. This smoke rising from the incense covered his eyes from a direct view of God. He also brought sacrificial blood with him to make atonement for sins (Exodus 28; Hebrews 9:7). Yet, no animal could be the perfect sacrifice and payment for our sins. No sacrifice was ever enough to tear the curtain that separated Israel and all of mankind from freely entering God's presence:

> The old system under the law of Moses was only a shadow, a dim preview of the good things to come, not the good things themselves. The sacrifices under that system were repeated again and again, year after year, but they were never able to provide perfect cleansing for those who came to worship. If they could have provided perfect cleansing, the sacrifices would have stopped, for the worshipers would have been purified once for all time, and their feelings of guilt would have disappeared. But instead, those sacrifices actually reminded them of their sins year after year. For it is not possible for the blood of bulls and goats to take away sins. That is why, when Christ came into the world, he said to God, "You did not want animal sacrifices or offerings. But You have given me a body to offer." . . . For God's will was for us to be made holy by the sacrifice of the body of Jesus Christ, once for all time. (**Heb. 10:1-5;10**)

Even with the barrier of sin between them, what does Exodus 33:11 tell us about Moses' relationship with God?

Jesus had not yet come to be the Perfect Sacrifice that removed the barrier between God and man. So what do you think verse 11 means when it says, "the Lord would speak to Moses face to face, as one speaks to a friend"?

Read Hebrews 11:24-27. What does this sat to you about the character of Moses?

In the Old Testament, the Bible says that Moses had a very deep relationship with God. Exodus 33:11 tells us that God spoke to him like a friend. This relationship was built through sustained time with God. Long periods of uninterrupted time. The result? He brilliantly reflected God's glory.

Let's learn from Moses' example. How does being aware of the Presence of God change us?

- **The more we spend time with God, the more we are aware of our own unworthiness and need for Him.**

  What does Numbers 12:3 tell us about Moses?

  Read Exodus 34:29-35. Earlier in this chapter, Moses had spent 40 days with God. This is when God gave Moses the Ten Commandments and outlined the Old Covenant. The Old Covenant was God's promise or agreement with the Israelites. If they obeyed His standards, they would be blessed. If they did not, they would experience His wrath.

  When Moses came down from the mountain, what did he look like?

  Why do you think Aaron and the Israelites were afraid?

Being aware of God's character and goodness (His glory) has a way of making us more aware of our sinfulness. We see the great contrast between His holy nature and our sinful one. Just like Adam and Eve, we are acutely aware of our nakedness before a holy God. Before Jesus came, that awareness was crushing.

- **The more time we spend with God, the more we draw from His power.**

   Read Exodus 34:28. How long did Moses go without food and water when he spent time with the Lord?

   Now let's look at this remarkable parallel. **Read Mark 4:1-11.** How long did Jesus fast before Satan came to tempt Him?

   Jesus had spent time in prayer and fasting with God. And although He was hungry, He was not weak. He was able to withstand the face-to-face tempting of Satan himself. Bearing in mind how long Moses went without food and water, take a moment to Google "How long can a person survive without water?" Write down what you find.

   Instead of emerging from this time sickly (or dead!), after time spent in deep, sustained communication with God, Moses exhibited God's glory so brightly that the Israelites and Aaron were afraid!

   His time away with God did not put him behind in his progress in God's plan and purpose for him. It energized him and equipped him! It does the same for us.

Read Jeremiah 2:13 and 17:13. How is God described in these verses? What does God say will happen when they do not refresh themselves with Him?

I'm not suggesting a 40-day fast of this type. What I *am* saying is this: Long periods of uninterrupted time with God empower us! We think we always have to be busy and doing. In truth, the most empowering thing we can do each day is focus on spending time with God — praying, reading His Word, sharing our struggles, asking for His direction. Our time with Him multiplies His power through us in ways that enable us to accomplish far more while doing far less.

The more time I spend with God, the shorter my "to-do" list has become. He has cleared so many things that were unnecessary and draining to me on all levels. He's given me courage to let go of good things, so I could make room for His best for me. And yet I see Him working through me more powerfully than during those many years of working myself to exhaustion.

Most people want us to be dependent so they can take power *from* us. God wants us to be dependent so He can give power *to* us!

- **The more time we spend with God, the more we love others.**

For years, I walked around bleeding, searching for people, things, and circumstances to heal my gaping wounds. I didn't trust God's love for me enough to believe that He truly wanted to heal my mind, heart, and body.

As I began to open my heart and let Him heal those wounded places, I have found that my love for others and my desire to serve them has steadily grown. It is difficult to address others' woundedness when we are still wounded ourselves. When we allow God's love to repair our wounded hearts, He empowers us to be a conduit of healing for others.

> We love because He first loved us. (**1 John 4:19**)

Throughout their 40-year journey in the wilderness, the Israelites were no easy crew. They complained often and continually accused Moses of leading them into the wilderness to die. Yet Moses was able to continually love and serve the people God had entrusted to Him.

As we discussed earlier, Moses experienced an amazing relationship with God, yet he didn't have *continual* access to His presence. Jesus' death and resurrection made that possible for us. We can now go to God at any time, with all of our joys, concerns, and feelings. We may *feel* alone at times, but we never have to *be* alone. God's presence is always accessible.

the Doctor can see you now

It's the phrase we all long to hear as we sit in the waiting room at the doctor's office: "The doctor can see you now." Before Jesus came, we were stuck in the waiting room. Waiting for access to the Treatment for our sinful condition. Waiting to have face-to-face relationship with the Great Physician.

We were in the waiting room desperately needing Someone to pull back the curtain between us and God the Father. We needed Someone to be the perfect, once-and-for-all sacrifice for our sins. Jesus came and died for our sins. He *is* that Someone. His perfect sacrifice satisfied the payment for our sins. When Jesus died, the curtain was pulled back. And He said the words we were longing to hear: "The Doctor can see you now."

> And so, dear brothers and sisters, we can boldly enter heaven's Most Holy Place because of the blood of Jesus. By his death, Jesus opened a new and life-giving way through the curtain into the Most Holy Place. And since we have a great High Priest who rules over God's house, let us go right into the presence

> of God with sincere hearts fully trusting him. For our guilty consciences have been sprinkled with Christ's blood to make us clean, and our bodies have been washed with pure water. **(Hebrews 10:19-22)**

Read Matthew 27:45-51. Maybe you already knew all about the history behind the temple veil. Maybe you're learning about it for the first time. Regardless, how do you feel when you read that passage?

Ladies, we are more than His wounded patient in need of Treatment. We are His bride. At a wedding, the bride wears a veil. When she is united with her groom, the veil is lifted and she turns toward him. In 2 Corinthians 3:16, Paul tells us, "But whenever someone turns to the Lord, the veil is taken away." When the veil is lifted, it allows for intimacy! We are His bride. He is our Groom.

Read Hebrews 4:13-16. What does verse 14 refer to Jesus as?

How does that have more meaning now that you perhaps have a better understanding of the role of the high priest in the Holy of Holies?

Hebrews 4:13 tells us we are exposed — naked — before a holy God. Satan wants us to process this as shame. **No!** The Law — all those rules and regulations — was meant to open our eyes to how sick we are. We can't possibly live up to God's standards perfectly. The Law was meant to make us realize our need for a Savior. **Look up Romans 7:6-7** and write it below:

Once that Savior came and died for us, we are no longer sick without access to the Treatment. The Doctor can see us now! And not so He can condemn us. He wants to see us to make us well. His presence is healing. You can't get closer the Healer without experiencing some measure of healing.

We aren't naked anymore. We are now clothed by the blood of Jesus. God sees us now as He sees His own Son! Hebrews 4:16 says, "So let us come boldly to the throne of our gracious God. There we will receive his mercy, and we will find grace to help us when we need it most."

For most of my life, I knew in my head that I had access to the merciful Doctor. I just didn't know it in my heart. So I would sheepishly approach Him and cower in fear and shame.

2 Corinthians 3:17 tells us, "For the Lord is the Spirit, and wherever the Spirit of the Lord is, there is freedom." We can approach God freely. There is no veil! Praise You, Jesus! This is not liberty to sin and do whatever we want. It's liberty from the overwhelming power sin had on our lives. We now have the Holy Spirit residing *in* us. When Jesus left earth, He left His Holy Spirit with us. When we accept Jesus as Savior, the Holy Spirit becomes a constant energizing internal voice and force that continually reminds us of God's truth and gives us the power to act on it. We will always struggle with sin, but it doesn't have to rule our lives!

Paul tells us exactly this in Romans 6:6: "We know that our old sinful selves were crucified with Christ so that sin might lose its power in our lives. We are no longer slaves to sin."

The more time we spend in God's Word and in communication with Him, the more we are transformed. That is what happened to Moses *before* Jesus came and died for us. How much greater it is for us now that we can see the Physician face-to-face!

> So all of us who have had that veil removed can see and reflect the glory of the Lord. And the Lord—who is the Spirit—makes us more and more like him as we are changed into his glorious image. (**2 Cor. 3:18**)

Let's look at 1 Corinthians 13:12. In essence, it says that we see Jesus dimly here on earth. If the veil has been lifted, why do you think Paul would say this?

Read 1 John 3:2. How does this verse perhaps help us understand?

The more we are aware of God's presence and read His Word, the more we sense His overwhelming love for us. But this journey of being more aware and in tune with God's presence is a journey we will be on for the rest of our lives. We are still human. Sin still clouds our view of God. We won't truly experience God in all His glory until we reach heaven. But how we see God today, and our increasing awareness of Him, prepares us for heaven when we will see Him as He is! Perfectly!

blinded to our Treatment

Let's think back to earlier in this lesson when we explored the questions that Satan sometimes asks us, the statements and lies he pelts us with as he tries to convince us that we should still be naked and ashamed.

Satan knows the veil has been lifted. Jesus tore it in two when He died and rose again. It can't be sewn back together. Jesus made sure of that, once and for all. So what is Satan's tactic? He tries to warp our perception. He is constantly trying to make us think we're still in the waiting room! To make us feel ashamed. To block our awareness of our access to our loving and all-powerful God.

I'll say it again: We *aren't* naked, ladies. When we accept Jesus as our Savior, we are clothed with the blood of Jesus Christ. No matter what we do or don't do, nothing can ever make us naked again.

There's another reason that Satan tries to put the veil back in place in our minds. He knows that the more we see of God and the more we experience His love for us, the more we will love Him and trust Him. He can still bombard us with those questions and lies we talked about earlier, but they won't have the same power because we've experienced the love of God for ourselves. We may not understand God's ways, but we know without a shadow of a doubt that He loves us. Even Satan knows how powerful that is.

As we begin to experience His love for us more and more, we follow His leading and He proves Himself faithful. This brings what we know of God in our heads into our hearts. These are not just *words* in the Bible. What the Bible says becomes true in our daily lives. This is powerful! It gives us a first-hand experience that we want to share with others. It moves us from saying, "I've heard that God is a good Doctor" to "The Great Physician healed me. Let me tell you about what He did for me." A personal testimonial is always more credible and powerful than just mere concepts that we haven't tested ourselves.

When we don't understand our position with God, we often unconsciously try to hide like Adam and Eve did. We hide in alcohol, drugs, distraction, and performance. They numb us. And keep us from seeing Who God really is. We want to hide from our perception of His piercing glare, when what He wants to show us is His piercing love.

When you're sick and need of a good doctor, you'll do anything you can to see him or her. Over the last two chapters, we've talked about the amazing credentials and skill of our loving Physician. He's calling us into His office. The Doctor will see you now.

The question now is this: *How badly do we want to see Him?*

your heart rewired

What truths or statements about God's character from this week's lesson do you most need embedded in your heart? **Write them here and meditate on them throughout the week:**

a heart rewired

the woman with the issue of blood

Read Mark 5:25-34. I can so relate to the story in Mark 5 of the poor woman with the issue of blood. Over the years, one of my many recurring ailments was chronic anemia due to blood loss. I made countless trips to the hematologist for iron infusions. I can tell you from personal experience that this condition takes such a toll on all levels. Overwhelming, to-the-bone exhaustion. Heavy mental fog. Even the smallest tasks are draining.

It was even more devastating for this dear woman. In Jewish culture, during a woman's period, she was considered "unclean." Anything she touched was unclean. Anyone she touched was considered unclean. This meant she could not worship at the synagogue. She could not participate in the normal rhythms of Jewish life. She likely was cut off from her family. It had probably been many years since she had experienced the warmth of human touch. This woman had tried every possible avenue for healing. She had spent every dollar and was no better off. She saw no way out of her physical and emotional misery.

How do you think her condition and restrictions impacted her emotionally and spiritually?

This woman went to Jesus when she was out of money and out of options. She realized He was her only hope. Mark 5:29 (KJV) tells us that her physical body was healed immediately: "And straightway the fountain of her blood was dried up; and she felt in her body that she was healed of that plague."

Immediately. The second she touched Jesus' robe. But I believe her spiritual and emotional healing may have started with a question. What question did Jesus ask in Mark 5:30? If Jesus knows everything, why do you think He might have asked this question?

There are probably a number of reasons, but I believe that simple question brought this hurting woman out of the shadows. Remember, this woman's bleeding made her and anyone who she touched unclean. If she had been allowed to simply be physically healed, then slink away unnoticed, what problems might have occurred?

This woman came to Jesus for physical healing. But her wounds went much deeper than the physical. According to Strong's Exhaustive Concordance of the Bible, the Greek word for "plague" in Mark 5:29 (KJV) is *mastix*, which means "a whip (lit. the Roman flagellum for criminals; fig. a disease) plague, scourging."[3] This conveys the idea of repeated, painful attack.

I understand this so well! Since I was in my mid-20s, I have suffered with ailments which improved for a time, but then, just when I thought I might be free of them, they'd strike me again. Trauma is cumulative.

Each trauma builds on the last, beating your mind, heart, and body down a little further each time. You begin to think you deserve it somehow. You become afraid to hope. You begin to accept defeat.

This is how Satan often works. He allows us to believe healing might be in sight, only to strike us down again. He wants us to give up hope. To accept defeat. Jesus wants us to realize, as this woman did, that *He* is our only hope. As crazy as it sounds, desperation can give us hope. It can strip us of all our confidence in circumstantial security and solutions, and drive us to the feet of our only true Hope, Jesus Christ.

Although Jesus can and does use doctors, diets, counselors, and other methods in our healing, He wants us to come to *Him* for guidance. *He* is the only One who knows exactly what our minds, hearts, and bodies need. When we come to the Healer, instead of grasping at straws and being no better off than when we started, we can then be gently led by Him to those people and methods He knows are ideally suited to our unique physical, emotional, and spiritual needs. As we focus on Him, His healing power begins to flow through us. Who could possibly know what we need better than our Creator?

The healing Jesus offers is always more than skin deep. This woman may have been invisible to others for years. But Jesus wanted her to know that *He* saw her pain. He wanted to publicly acknowledge to the crowd who had shunned her that she was healed. She was clean! He wanted to relieve her of the many years of shame and isolation she had endured.

This woman's story also gives us encouragement that no matter how long we have struggled with an issue, no matter how hopeless it may seem, it doesn't hinder God's ability to heal and restore us.

a new view of God: the key to a whole new heart

Your eye is like a lamp that provides light for your body. When your eye is healthy, your whole body is filled with light. But when it is unhealthy, your body is filled with darkness. (**Luke 11:34**)

We often don't let go of our own efforts and ways of healing our minds, hearts, and bodies until we run out of options. It is then that we can recognize that Jesus is our only Hope. As we make the CHOICE to believe that Jesus is our only Hope, and take ACTION to reach for Him instead of our own remedies, He will show us the way forward.

Vision Clouded by Lies: She believes she is invisible, as if no one sees her. She believes she has to figure out her own healing path, but she can't. She believes she's tried everything.

Choice: Despite all her disappointments, she chose to believe that Jesus could help her."For she thought to herself, 'If I can just touch his robe, I will be healed.'" (Mark 5:28)

Action: She went to Jesus, risking being scorned and punished as she moved through the crowd making others "unclean."

The Clear Lens of Love: *Jesus* sees her! *Sigh*. She can rest. God knows everything going on in her life. She is not alone.

Result: She was healed. She was no longer ostracized. Jesus called her Daughter.

> *When Jesus saw him lying there and learned that he had been in this condition for a long time, he asked him, 'Do you want to get well?'*
> **(John 5:6 NIV)**

In Week One, I told you about my friend Ann's heart problems. During a hospital stay, one of her doctors spoke bluntly to her in a way that she believes saved her life.

This is what Ann told me: "She (the doctor) came into my room, looked at my chart and simply said, 'Ann, people like you frustrate me. We do all we can do to help you to be well and you don't do your part.'"

It wasn't easy to hear, but she says it was finally the jolt she needed. "I wasn't disciplined with my eating. I didn't like to walk, so I didn't — at least not consistently. Even though I knew these things were important. Even though I knew they would make me feel better. This recent bout with heart problems was painful and scary enough to get my attention. I wanted to live. My sister got me a FitBit® for Christmas, and I started walking her dog. And guess what? I started to *enjoy* walking ... I weigh less than I have in 20 years! At 81 years old, my heart is doing great and I feel fantastic."

My friend Ann had the keys to health and healing all along. It was always accessible to her. For years, her doctors had told her what she had needed to do to be well. She *knew* what she needed to do. But she experienced the benefits only when she began to make regular and deliberate *choices* to follow the treatment.

Medical doctors give us prescriptions for health, but they don't force us to take them. It's not a command. It's simply an invitation: "I have a treatment that will bring you life. You're invited to come and try it." It's ultimately our *choice* whether to consent to the treatment. If we don't, we will suffer consequences. It's not because the doctor is punishing us, but simply because when we don't follow the treatment, we can't experience its benefits.

Ann's healing is an *ongoing* process as she makes daily choices. Continual choices to follow the treatment. We have a choice, too. Like Ann, we have to decide how badly we want to be well. How badly do we desire the true wellness of our mind, heart, and body that comes from getting to the root of the problem — our diseased hearts — and taking the right treatment?

It seems like the answer should be easy, but let's face it: The path to true wellness is often painful. Healthy choices take discipline and require us to let go of things — even good things — that we are depending upon for our worth and security. We may have to let go of old thought patterns, beliefs, and unhealthy relationships. We have to let go of *our* way of doing things.

As our Great Physician, God sent His Son to die for us to bring us life and healing. We don't have to earn it. We just have to receive Jesus' death as payment for our sins. It gives us 24/7 access to our Heavenly Father — the Great Physician. *He* is the treatment. He doesn't just *give us* the treatment. He *is* the Treatment. The Treatment for our diseased hearts.

Healing isn't an instant process. It involves making choices to heighten our awareness of the presence of God. His love, His wisdom, His leading, and His power gives us the strength and discernment to address those areas of our hearts that are making us sick — unhealthy relationships, destructive habits and thought patterns. Only He knows what is holding us back from the peace, joy, and rest He freely offers. We just so often forget to regularly and continually consult the Doctor and follow the Treatment.

The more we make deliberate, intentional choices to be aware of His presence, the more we will experience heart health. We find joy, peace, love, and rest. He *is* all those things. And as I've said numerous times before, it is impossible to get closer to the Treatment without receiving some measure of healing. That will look different for each of us. Jesus never healed the same way twice in the Gospels. He met each person in a way that He knew would reveal the sickness and wounding of each heart and heal his or her very unique mind and body. A way only He truly knew because He created him or her. They thought their greatest need was physical healing, but God knew it went far deeper. They needed to open their hearts to the Savior of their souls. He wanted to heal their hearts. He wants to heal ours, too. But we have to make the choice to receive it. To walk in it. Daily. Moment by moment. Choice by choice.

read and reflect

When our human hearts are sick, we experience symptoms like racing heartbeat, shortness of breath, dizziness, and chest pain. When our spiritual hearts are sick, we experience symptoms too: Destructive anger, fear, discouragement, shame . . . just to name a few.

So often we focus on trying to control the *symptoms* in our lives. We concentrate on strategies to be less fearful, less discouraged, less angry, less prideful. We make some progress in one or more of these areas, but then find ourselves entangled again. We need to focus on the Treatment — Jesus — not the symptoms, or we never truly get well. Jesus knows what is at the root of our fear, discouragement, anger, and pride. As we focus on Him and allow Him to treat the root causes, our symptoms will become less and less frequent. They may never completely disappear (we're human, after all), but they won't dominate our lives. Jesus and His healing power will.

I think Jesus says something like this to us: "I want to simplify it for you, Daughter. *Just focus on Me*. Make choices that heighten your awareness of My Presence. I AM the Treatment. I am the Bread of Life, the Living Water. As you make choices to focus on Me and follow My leading, you will experience My healing. Day by day, moment by moment. And you'll experience joy, rest, and peace like you've never known. I promise. And I'm known to keep My word. In fact, I'm the only One who has a perfect track record. The Treatment is always accessible. I never withhold it."

We *need* the Treatment. Not just once. We need a continual flow of the healing power of the Great Physician. The path to wellness will not be easy. It is a dying to self. It will require difficult and painful things of us. *But so does living without the Treatment.* At least when we are following the Treatment, we know the pain is leading to a deeper level of spiritual, mental, and emotional health. It's leading to a greater and sweeter awareness of God's love and rest. It's pain that leads to healing, not more sickness.

Ironically, as we begin to experience the outcomes we have always been dreaming of — joy, peace, rest —we realize that those things are not an outcome at all. They are a *Person*. The more we are aware of His presence and choose to communicate and partner with Him, the more we experience all those things.

symptom management

What are some of your most troublesome "symptoms" — fear, discouragement, anger, impatience, selfishness? How have you been trying to "treat" them? Take a few minutes and Google "Bible verses about fear" (or whichever symptoms you struggle with most). Write the verse or verses below that impact you the most.

When we experience these symptoms, it's a good reminder to refocus on God. Awareness of His life-giving, loving presence begins to make them recede. Not overnight. But step by step. Choice by God-led choice. We are taking the Treatment.

For most of my life, I was playing Whac-a-Mole® with the symptoms of my physical and heart sickness. Whac-a-Mole® is a game in which a number of moles begin to pop up from various holes at random. The object of the game is to force the individual moles back into their holes by hitting them on the head with a mallet. The quicker you do this, the higher your score.

I was often far more focused on trying to control the "moles" — the symptoms of my heart condition — than on the Treatment. As soon as I got one symptom to subside, another one would pop up. I became exhausted through my own efforts and wisdom to get well. But I wasn't sure I could trust the Treatment. I was afraid the Treatment might kill me (literally!). Or that He would require things of me that I didn't know if I could — or wanted — to give Him. Ultimately, I had to answer the question Jesus poses to each of us: "Do *you* want to get well?"

Getting well often means we have to let go of our tendency to see ourselves as victims. We have to give up convenient or comfortable excuses for our attitudes and behavior. We have to be willing to let go of certain mindsets and beliefs. Getting well is painful. It can also be *frightening*. At least dysfunction is familiar. It might be unhealthy, but at least we know what to expect. On some warped level, it feels safe.

I think about my mom. She had such a tender heart, caring spirit, deep love for God and other people, not to mention a wonderful, quirky sense of humor and infectious laugh. But her life was, in many ways, incredibly tragic. Her parents divorced when she was two years old. Her mother died suddenly when she was six. Her father was physically and emotionally absent for most of her childhood. One of the family members who primarily helped raise her was often manipulative, abusive, and narcissistic.

My mom learned to cope through a variety of unhealthy "medications" — food, performance, people-pleasing. At the age of 65, she had a psychotic break and was diagnosed with bipolar disorder. One night, I found myself admitting my mom into a behavioral health center for treatment. By God's grace, the director of the facility was a godly and compassionate man. He and his team gave my mom every possible tool to help her get well. And yet, I'll never forget what the director told me: "Melinda, I know God can do amazing things. But what I have seen so often is that when a person's illness has gone untreated for this long, they often don't ever get well. They've become too used to the dysfunction. It is just too scary and overwhelming to change."

Sadly, that was the case with my mom. She made brave steps toward healing, but then eventually shut down when the pain, opposition, and difficulty became too great. Four years later, she died of ovarian cancer. She knew Jesus as Savior. I know I will see her in heaven one day. Jesus saved her soul, but I believe He wanted her to experience a deeper level of healing and wellness while she was here on earth. I believe He desires that for each of us.

our hearts need rest

> I have cared for you since you were born. Yes, I carried you before you were born. I will be your God throughout your lifetime—until your hair is white with age. I made you, and I will care for you. I will carry you along and save you. (**Isaiah 46:3-4**)

Recently, I went to the airport to pick up my husband from a trip to visit family. As I was waiting for his plane to arrive, I observed a father with a baby over his shoulder. This little one was blissfully limp and sound asleep. It struck me how entirely secure that child must have felt in his father's arms. Not alarmed that he was six feet off the ground. Unconcerned and oblivious to all the noise and chaos around him. That baby was just resting. Our Heavenly Father's greatest desire is for us to be like that child, trusting and resting secure in His love and care for us.

God's heart longs for you to *be continually aware of His presence*. That is where our security is found. When that happens, we are aware of His very tender, personal love for us. The more we are aware of that love, the more our hearts change. It's in that place that we know to the core of our being that we can trust Him. Awareness of His love is inspiring. It inspires us to serve not because we *have* to, but because we *want* to — out of our love for Him, not out of obligation.

As we discussed in Week Three, we have no reason to feel shame. Jesus took our guilt and shame on the cross, so we could be free. Free to rest in knowing that we don't have to earn our salvation. We don't have to worry and fret and obsess over our futures and our circumstances. We just have to follow Him. Where and how He leads will challenge, stretch, and sometimes cause us pain. He didn't promise an easy journey. But He did promise to never leave us or forsake us (Deut. 31:6 NIV).

When we connect more and more to His presence, we realize what an incredible gift that is. We can rest in knowing that His leading is always guided by His overwhelming love for us, even if it doesn't always look or feel like it. We don't have to *earn* that rest, but we do have to *choose* it.

We have to choose to walk in His grace and love. This is not a one-time choice. It is a one-step, one-decision, one-moment at-a-time way of living.

> **This is my heartfelt prayer for each of us:**
>
> ... may you have the power to understand, as all God's people should, how wide, how long, how high, and how deep his love is. May you experience the love of Christ, though it is too great to understand fully. Then you will be made complete with all the fullness of life and power that comes from God. (**Eph. 3:18-19**)

As we discussed earlier, we often focus on the symptoms, not the Treatment. We focus on trying to have joy, to be patient, to persevere. But without a moment-by-moment, deep, abiding relationship with God, we will find ourselves endlessly frustrated. Able to make improvement, experiencing glimpses or seasons of it, but not truly finding the lasting, healing transformation we crave. Transformation can only occur through a *heart* knowledge of the goodness and love of God. It is the result of making continual, intentional choices to act on His Word and promises and remind ourselves of His love and goodness. As we do, we'll grow in our knowledge of Him as our Source of peace, joy, love, rest, and so much more.

We often think of rest as a physical condition. How would you describe mental rest? Spiritual rest?

Have you experienced spiritual or mental rest before — even for brief periods? What do you attribute it to?

Read Hebrews 4:1-3. In Hebrews 3, Paul writes about how God had led Israel out of Egypt so He could lead them into the Promised Land. He would be their God and provide them with gifts and joy and rest beyond their imagination. All they had to do was follow God's lead. It was approximately a 240-mile journey that could have been negotiated in a matter of weeks, even by foot. Instead, as we know, they wandered in the wilderness for 40 years. Most of them died there, never entering the rest that God had promised.

What kind of rest do you think Hebrews 4 is speaking of? Rest from what?

Read Hebrews 3:19. Why didn't most of the Israelites experience the rest that God promised them?

Look up and write down the definition of "unbelief."

Now look up the definition of "doubt."

How do you think that unbelief differs from doubt?

Now let's look at Numbers 13:27-33 and 14:10. Moses had sent 12 spies to stake out the Promised Land before they entered. What did they see when they arrived there?

How did it compare with what God told them the Promised Land would look like (Exodus 3:17)?

Joshua and Caleb believed that they could enter the Promised Land. What was the response of the other 10 spies (v. 31-32)? How did the unbelief of these spies affect the Israelites? (13:32 & 14:1-4)

Look at Deuteronomy 11:22-28. Considering the promises that God made to Israel, how does Israel's response to entering Canaan strike you?

The obstacle to their rest was deeper than simply fear of the giants in Canaan. Over and over again, the Israelites rebelled against God and went their own way. *They had a problem of the heart.* They didn't believe God's promises. They didn't want to do things His way. In Deut. 11:26-28, God tells Israel, "You will be blessed if you obey the commands of the Lord your God . . . But you will be cursed if you reject the commands of the Lord your God . . ."

Today, because of Jesus' sacrifice on the cross, we live under God's grace, not the Law of reward and punishment. But the principle of *choice* is still the same. God says to us today, "You don't have to *earn* My rest. It is freely available to you. But I'm not going to force it on you. I've given you a free will. If you choose to believe and rest in My love and My presence — despite all the giants in your life, despite your desire to go your own way — you will experience incredible rest and peace. If not, just like Israel, you will wander in the wilderness, but not because I'm punishing you. It's because lasting rest and peace is just not possible without a regular awareness and deeper knowledge of Who I am. And I am Love. If you trust Me and follow Me, you will find rest for your mind, heart, and body."

We'd like to think we are different than the Israelites. But are we? Aren't we just as stubborn? Just as determined to do things our way? Don't we struggle to believe God's promises? To believe He is trustworthy when our circumstances tell us a different story? I know I do!

Below, let's look at some promises of God. Look up the Scripture and write the promise. Then write what choice (if any) each verse says we can make to experience (not *earn*) that promise.

Promises of God

Matthew 6:33

Matthew 11:28 30

Philippians 4:6-7

Philippians 1:6

Romans 8:28

Psalm 37:4

Over the next four weeks, we'll be looking at four biblical "REST principles" that we can apply to our lives: **R**educe Distractions, **E**at from the Feast of God's Word, **S**urrender to His Love, and **T**rust Him Step-by-Step. *This is not a formula.* God hates formulas (and so do I!). Our tendency is to look to formulas for direction and success instead of to God. What works for one person may not work for someone else. Formulas deny God's creativity and uniqueness in dealing with His children. REST is *not* a formula. These are simply *principles* that create an environment for the Holy Spirit to open our eyes to His powerful and loving presence. To reveal and heal our hearts. Principles are core or foundational truths. As we make choices to follow these principles, He will lovingly and powerfully reveal Himself and His plan and purpose for each person in a way that is unique and personal.

While this is not about formulas, it's also not about following rules. It's not about "if I do this, God will do this." No! That is Old Testament thinking! His standards still remain, but we are under grace. Praise Jesus! We no longer have to *earn* anything.

It isn't about earning. It's about *choosing*. We are given a free will. Our will can free us as we make choices to seek Him! Gradually, He opens our eyes. He's so patient. It's a gradual revelation. He's a patient Healer. He gradually peels back layers of the heart one at a time, as He knows we are ready for it.

Every habit feels difficult and unnatural at first. It's just like when you first begin exercising or going to the gym. For the first few weeks, you have to drag yourself there. But eventually, you start to experience the benefits: renewed health, renewed energy, renewed focus. And although it still takes intentional discipline, you have now *experienced* the benefits of that discipline. And you want more. You don't just know in your head that you should exercise. You've persevered long enough to know in your heart that it is worth the cost. I have personally found this also applies to the "REST principles" we'll be exploring in the next four chapters.

God's love, His presence, His provision, His resources are all right there. All completely accessible. His resources are limitless. His love knows no bounds. Victory, not just in heaven, but right here on earth, is entirely available and possible.

your heart rewired

What truths or statements about God's character from this week's lesson do you most need embedded in your heart? **Write them here and meditate on them throughout the week:**

a heart rewired

the man at the pool of bethesda

Read John 5:1-9. Briefly describe the scene in this passage. Put yourself at the Pool of Bethesda that day. Specifically record the mood, the sights, the smells, the sounds you might have observed and experienced if you were there.

Verse 5 tells of a specific invalid who was there that day. How long had this man been paralyzed? Based on that, describe what you think this man's emotional condition might have been when Jesus approached him.

Verse 6 (NIV) says that Jesus saw him lying there and "learned that he had been in this condition for a long time." Jesus — the King of questions (who actually knows *everything*) — most likely asked others around the paralytic more about this man. What does this tell you about the nature and heart of Jesus?

What question does Jesus ask the man in verse 6? Does this seem like an odd question to you? Why?

Considering what we've studied in this week's lesson so far, why do you think Jesus asked it?

Look at verse 7. Consider deeply the man's response. How might it reflect his fears and mindset?

It makes me think of how we are all like this paralyzed man. We look to everything else to heal us, while the Healer stands right in front of us.

We don't dare hope that the healing Jesus offers is real. We often limit God to what we believe is possible in our own minds and in our own power. It protects us from disappointment.

This point is emphasized by the location where this healing took place. According to verse 2, it took place in Bethesda which means "house of mercy." What does it say Bethesda was near?

Now look at John 10:7&9. What might be the connection between what Jesus says in those verses and why He chose to heal this man at this location?

The man said that he had "no one to put me into the pool" (v.7). Notice that Jesus didn't pick him up and carry him to the water. Instead, He said, "Get up! Pick up your mat and walk." (v.8 NIV) It was the man's *choice*. Jesus wanted to *partner* with this man in his healing process. When we partner with God, it builds trust and relationship. What would you have thought of Jesus' instructions if you were this man?

In verse 9, it tells us that regardless of what the man may have thought of what Jesus told him to do, the man obeyed. What do you think prompted a man who had been paralyzed for 38 years to obey the instructions of a man he didn't even know?

Jesus didn't tell this man to heal himself. God doesn't ask us to heal ourselves either. He just asks us to follow Him. Our willingness to do so reflects how badly we truly want to get well.

What God asks of us on our path to wellness might not make sense to us. At times, his instructions might even seem cruel. (Who asks a lame man to pick up his mat and walk?!) We might not always understand His ways, but we can always trust His heart.

After his miraculous healing, Jesus slips away. The man didn't fully know who Jesus was, but he clearly believed this Man was worth his attention and obedience. But John 5:14 shows us that Jesus was concerned about this man's spiritual health, not just his physical well-being: "But afterward Jesus found him in the Temple and told him, "Now you are well; so stop sinning, or something even worse may happen to you." (v.14)

Jesus told the man this because He knows that sin — decisions to do things our way instead of God's way — makes us sick. It's not because God is punishing us. It's simply because choices that go against what God intended for our good have natural consequences. He wanted this man to make choices that would bring him life.

a new view of God: the key to a whole new heart

> *Your eye is like a lamp that provides light for your body. When your eye is healthy, your whole body is filled with light. But when it is unhealthy, your body is filled with darkness.* (**Luke 11:34**)

We so often see the barriers to our healing, rather than focusing on the Healer who is right there in front of us. He may ask us to do things that don't make sense to us. It's our choice to follow His leading. But if we are willing to trust Him, we will see and experience His faithfulness and love in ways that we didn't think were possible. It is our CHOICE to trust Him and open our minds and hearts to Him. If we do, our new view of Him will spur us to ACTION — walking daily with Him on a new path of victory, healing, and freedom.

Vision Clouded by Lies: This condition is beyond help. He will always live in this paralyzed, crippled condition. There is no hope.

Choice: Even though all hope of healing seems foolish and impossible from a human standpoint, he chooses to believe that being made well is possible.

The Clear Lens of Love: Hope is right in front of him! It's not a pool. It's a Person.

Action: He followed Jesus' instructions to "Pick up your mat and walk." (John 5:8 NIV)

Result: The man was healed of his 38-year condition, reminding us that the length of our problem is not a barrier to God's ability to heal.

Medical Prescription Form

Rx

Patient Information

Patient name : .... You ....

Patient address : ....

Directions:

Reduce Distractions
Eat from the Feast of My Word
Surrender to My Love
Trust Me Step by Step

Signature ..... *God* .....
Date ..... Everyday .....

> *[Spiritual rest] . . . is not a hallowed feeling that comes over us in church. It is . . . the eternal calm of an invulnerable faith, the repose of a heart set deep in God.*
> ~ **Henry Drummond** [4]

No matter what the physical ailment, rest is often part of the prescription. Why? Rest is restorative. It promotes healing of the body. It's also vital for healing the heart and mind.

The Great Physician prescribes continual rest for you and me. Even when that's not possible physically, we can rest in Him. We can rest when we *remember* that He loves us passionately and will never leave us or forsake us. We can rest *remembering* that no matter what we've done, we can speak honestly and boldly to God without shame because Jesus paid the price for our sins. The enemy does everything he can to break our awareness of the amazing love and power of God. He knows that when we forget God's love, power, and goodness, rest is quickly replaced by fear, worry, and overwhelm.

So how do we know if we're resting? Here's how I've experienced it:

- **An inward calm and peace** regardless of circumstances.

- **A settled trust that I don't have to figure it all out** and work myself to exhaustion because I know my Father is always working and always working *for my good*.

- **An assurance that I don't have to make things happen.** As I choose to focus my mind on God with my prayers, thoughts, needs and requests, and trust and follow His leading, I know in my heart that He will open the right doors for me at the right time. I'm confident that He can make connections and provision that I could never have orchestrated or even thought of!

Ultimately, I can rest because I am secure in God. My security and identity doesn't lie in busyness, status, achievement, others' opinions, or my ability to get everything right. Those things change constantly. When I accept Jesus' sacrifice as payment for my sins, I am His valuable, dearly loved child forever. My value in His eyes *never* changes.

remember to rest

We don't have to earn the rest God freely offers. But we do have to intentionally pursue it. It doesn't just "happen." We have to *remember* to rest! It doesn't come easily or naturally. People, politics, media, and circumstances are all too happy to steal our ability to rest if we aren't actively pursuing and protecting it.

Studying and applying the following biblical REST principles lead us to the Treatment — the Great Physician. When we are in His "office," focused on Him, He reveals His love and wisdom in personal ways that soothe our hearts and minds. As we apply these principles, we open the door for the Holy Spirit to lead and work in our lives in ways that are uniquely tailored to our own needs, temperaments, and circumstances.

REST

Reduce Distractions

Eat from the Feast of God's Word

Surrender to His Love

Trust Him Step by Step

We need these life-changing REST principles to go down deeply into our hearts, so they can transform and heal us from the inside out. The Great Physician freely offers His healing to us. As we rest and trust in Him, it moves what we know in our heads into our hearts. However, He's given us free will. It's *our choice* — moment-by-moment — whether or not to follow the rest "prescription." *No one can rest for us.*

Are you ready for some cardiac rehab? Are you ready to REST? Healing always occurs from the inside out. Open your heart to the Ultimate Cardiologist.

> *If you look for me wholeheartedly,*
> *you will find me.*
> **(Jeremiah 29:13)**

As God began to expand my view of Him, I wanted more of this loving God that I was just beginning to know. He clearly put this thought in my mind: "If you want more of Me, you have to start consuming less of other things."

It didn't feel like a harsh command. It felt like a loving *invitation*. I knew immediately that I had to quit consuming so much media. At first it was difficult. Dozens of times a day, I fought impulses to pick up my phone or jump onto social media at every idle moment. This was uncharted territory for me.

My mind was far more used to racing to the next "to-do," the next text, the next email, the next project, the next news story. For the first time in forever, I began to allow my mind opportunities and room to just be (gasp!) *still*. A remarkable thing began to happen.

I saw God. *Everywhere*. No, not the Person of God, but His activity — His little messages of love, confirmations of things I was praying about. God began to become clearer and more compelling than the distractions. More compelling than anything I had ever experienced before. He truly became my Best Friend.

The brain is a muscle. The more we flex that muscle — training it to focus again and again on truth, on dialoguing with God, on praising Him, on focusing on His Word — it literally retrains our brains. We begin to be able to keep our minds focused, and in that place, for longer and longer without as much effort. What begins as a "hyper-awareness" of God that feels unnatural and exhausting, gives way to a Holy Spirit-led walk with the Best Doctor, the Best Friend we will ever have.

We can change the way we think by changing our focus. It takes time and discipline, but God designed it to be beautifully possible. Renewal and transformation of our minds and hearts is an ongoing process. But every time we focus on Jesus, our Healer, it renews our minds! This focus reminds us not just of the truth, but of the power, goodness, and love of Jesus, the Truth Giver.

Focusing on the distractions, however, keeps us from confronting the lies we believe and addressing the deeply buried wounds in our hearts and minds. Jesus is the Healer, the Great Physician. Satan wants to dull our awareness of God because he knows that the more we focus on Him, the more it brings healing! No matter what mistakes we've made, no matter how much shame and inadequacy we feel, we are loved. Nothing can change God's love for us. He is longing for us to seek Him. We'll find a depth of love we didn't know existed.

> Those who are dominated by the sinful nature think about sinful things, but those who are controlled by the Holy Spirit think about things that please the Spirit. So letting your sinful nature control your mind leads to death. But letting the Spirit control your mind leads to life and peace. (**Romans 8:5-6**)

what is distraction?

Distractions can be both internal and external. So often, I have been guilty of trying to "treat" the internal distractions — worry, fear, discouragement, shame, hidden wounds — without focusing on God, the Treatment. It's a useless effort because we can't treat ourselves. The only thing we can do is choose to reduce the *external* distractions that prevent us from seeing the Treatment clearly. As we do that, the Great Physician begins to heal the *internal* distractions that are holding us back from being truly well. God doesn't command us to focus on Him. He *invites* us.

It's a *loving* invitation. He knows that when we choose to train our focus on Him, we will continually be comforted and strengthened by His love. This is crucial, because so often our circumstances and emotions can be in conflict with Who God is. They can seem anything but loving. But this I know: Circumstances and emotions change. The love of God does not.

God doesn't just give us His love. He *is* Love. Whatever we choose to focus on becomes bigger in our minds and hearts. Since God *is* love, peace, joy, kindness, and goodness, when we begin to focus on Him more and more, all those things fill our minds and hearts in greater and greater measure. Our awareness of His power and overwhelming love for us becomes larger than our fear and doubt. Focusing on God doesn't make our problems suddenly disappear, but it does put them in a different perspective as we realize and remember His tender love, awesome power, and willingness to guide and provide for us throughout everything we face.

So *why* is it so hard to stay focused on Him? Well, in my case, I often have about a two-second attention span! Can anyone relate? I focus on God and think, "God, You are amazing. I know You are good and loving and wonderful. I can't believe I ever, ever forget or doubt that! Woo Hoo! Let's do this thing!"

And then, suddenly, I get distracted. Overwhelmed by life and tasks. And just like that, I'm immediately diverted into murky waters. Suddenly, I can't see God or remember anything about how amazing He is or how much He loves me. Or how much I love Him. I have to choose to go back to that Person who has introduced Himself to me a million times and get re-acquainted. God never gets exasperated with our constant memory lapses. He is always ready and waiting with open arms to make a loving re-introduction.

focusing on the "one thing"

Being distracted from Who and what is important is an age-old problem. **Let's look at Luke 10:38-42.** This may be a very familiar story to you. If so, ask God to help you read it with fresh eyes. There is much truth to be discovered in these four little verses.

We've probably all had the experience of preparing for a visit from someone we care about. **Describe the scene in these verses.** What can you imagine Martha was doing and thinking as she prepared for Jesus and the disciples to come to her home?

Contrast what Mary and Martha were doing in verses 39-40. Who was most at rest? Look carefully at verse 40. What do you think was the *"one thing"* that kept **Martha** from resting?

Martha came to Jesus upset. What did *she* think she needed to be at rest?

Martha believed she needed a change in circumstances to ease her anxious heart. What circumstances (either current or past) did/do *you* think need to change in order for *you* to be content?

What are the problems with expecting a change in circumstances to give us peace? What can we miss out on?

Martha most likely legitimately needed help. Was it wrong for her to ask for it? Why or why not?

Jesus responds to Martha in verse 41: "But the Lord said to her, 'My dear Martha, you are worried and upset over all these details!'"

Making preparations for Jesus and His disciples was a kind and generous act. And certainly, we all need help at times, as Martha did. Neither of those things are *wrong*. But earlier, we saw that Martha was *distracted*. How do you think her distraction led to her mental and emotional state found in verse 41? *What was she distracted from?*

What do you think the "one thing" is that Jesus says is needed in verse 42? How would you describe it?

Obviously, we can't spend all our time *literally* sitting still and focusing on Jesus. We have to live our lives. There is active work that God has called us to do. Preparing for Jesus and her other guests was, in itself, a good thing. However, it became a problem for Martha because her *serving of Jesus* drew her away from her focus on *being with Jesus*. Serving and doing shouldn't take us away from being with God. It should draw us closer to Him. The key is to ask God, "How can I partner with You today?" When our focus is on Jesus, He will show us what tasks and activities are most important. We will begin to sense His leading and His voice *as* we are doing and serving. He invites us to have an ongoing dialogue with Him as we partner together.

How can we be "sitting at the feet of Jesus" — focusing on Him in our hearts and minds as we go throughout the day? What could that look like for you personally?

How do you think that kind of focus on Jesus would impact your heart and mindset? Your behavior and choices?

All those years, when I was so distracted grasping for remedies to heal my heart, mind, and body, I believe this is what God wanted me to understand: "You only need one thing: You need *Me*. You need to see Me as I truly am. My love. My power. My goodness. I know you better than you know yourself. I created you. As you *choose* to delight in Me, over and over again, you'll find all your heart's desires, but perhaps not in the way you think. I am your Everything. And I won't disappoint. You just don't know it yet."

It's the message He gives to all of us: "You need one thing: *Me*."

your *heart* rewired

Rewiring our minds can seem like an overwhelming task. *It is.* In fact, it is impossible for us to do. Only God can embed truth and peace into our muddled, lie-ridden minds and hearts. Whatever small steps we take in His direction, He will run to meet us. The more we unclutter our minds of worry, planning, media, and other distractions, the more room we make for God to occupy our thoughts. We can't always change our circumstances, but we can change our *focus*.

Let's start this week by reducing the distractions we can control. As we do that, it will gradually become easier to keep our eyes on the "one thing" in the midst of distractions we *can't* control.

What distractions or habit(s) might God be inviting you to let go of so you can grasp the "one thing"? For example, one of my habits was to grab for my phone at any spare moment, starting from the moment I woke up in the morning. I began to fight that impulse and just allow my mind to be still. And I felt peace because there was finally room for God to fill it.

Write down your top three distractions below. Begin to intentionally and gradually reduce them, one by one. Remember: Change takes time and deliberate, repeated choices. Ask someone to keep you accountable.

Getting started is always the hardest part. As you begin to eliminate distractions, one day, one moment, one choice at a time, it *will* get easier.

> Don't copy the behavior and customs of this world, but let God transform you into a new person by changing the way you think. Then you will learn to know God's will for you, which is good and pleasing and perfect. (**Romans 12:2**)

Continual life application results in gradual heart transformation.

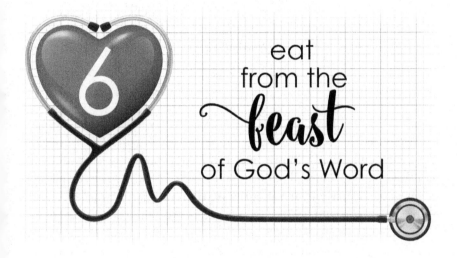

> *Taste and see that the Lord is good.*
> *Oh, the joys of those who*
> *take refuge in him!*
> (**Psalm 34:8**)

Reducing toxic food in our lives is an important step toward health. However, getting well requires more than *reducing* life-draining influences and distractions. It's about more than just *not* "eating" the wrong things. We also have to *fill* our minds and hearts with the right food. Just as regular consumption of whole, healthy foods is critical to our physical health, regular consumption of truth is also vital for us to thrive spiritually.

As God has healed my mind, heart, and body, I've been freed from years of restrictive medical diets. But I still try to eat with intention. I feel better when I take time to choose my foods wisely and plan for my meals. After many years of associating food with pain, I am slowly allowing God to show me how to develop a healthy relationship with food.

My relationship with God also felt very restrictive for most of my life — restricted by lies I've believed about Him, His character, and how He feels about me. After many years of associating God with displeasure and pain, I am allowing God to show me how to have a healthy relationship with *Him*.

He is the food for our hearts and minds. His Word is a life-giving love letter to us. As we read and savor our time with Him, He reveals to us more of Who He is. He communicates personally to us and builds relationship. He overwhelms our hearts with His love for us. When I'm not deliberate, consistent, and intentional about connecting with my loving Physician,

I start to feel heartsick again. Physical wellness is a journey. Spiritual wellness is also a journey. It takes time to detox the lies that have made us sick. It takes time and discipline to replace toxic beliefs, thoughts, and attitudes with healthy habits and beliefs. The Physician does the healing work. Our role is simply to choose to come to His office and follow His leading. Simple, but not always easy.

no time to eat?

Feasting on good food takes time and planning. But it slowly heals our hearts and minds. It doesn't leave us hungry. Think about fast food. Is it quick? *Yes.* Is it convenient? *Sure.* But does it really satisfy? Is it really what's *best*? Yet, so often we settle for picking up our nourishment at the drive-thru window.

Our pain has a way of making us hungry, not for food, but for God. We realize with a depth of clarity how truly sick we are: physically, emotionally, and spiritually.

I've been a "good" Christian girl for most of my life. But there were big questions that I had never really settled in my heart: *Did God truly love me? Was He really trustworthy?* I secretly and often questioned the depth of His love for me as I cried out in pain and agony while He remained silent. I fought exhausting invisible battles with doubt and anxiety. I was sick and still am in so many ways. *We all are.* It's a continual, ongoing process of going to God and asking Him to remove toxins that poison our hearts, minds, and bodies.

For many years, I had gone to Christian women's conferences, read lots of other people's inspiring experiences, and had done and led dozens and dozens of Bible studies. Those things are all helpful in growing our relationship with God. God has used them greatly in my life. I hope God uses this study in yours! But I came to a place where I was hungry for more than just what others said about God. I needed to know, for myself, Who He really was. I wanted to get well. Not just physically, but spiritually. My big nagging questions needed answers. And they could only be found with a deliberate, intentional, personal *study* of God's Word.

True study is not a "drive-thru" experience. I began to find answers to my questions as I chose to spend time soaking in God's Word day after day. And once those questions were answered, God continues to take me deeper still. He is bringing me to a place of completely depending on Him. Of being bold enough to trust Him, step by step, even when I don't know where He's leading me. Of laying down my dreams (some of which I've had since I was a little girl) and saying, "I only want what *You* want."

It often feels painful and scary. Over and over again, I have to ask Him to help me stay in this place. I often mess up and have to ask for His forgiveness and mercy. But that's exactly the point, isn't it? Allowing Him to empower us and guide us, moment by moment? That's what I'd been missing all these years.

Instead of going to Him with the goal of getting answers, plans, or comfort, I began to come to Him and simply say: "Lord, show me more of Who You are." I haven't rushed. I've feasted. I've waited in silence for Him to speak. Because eating is social. It's not just about nourishment. It's about *relationship*. You eat with family. You eat with friends.

I quit rushing through our time together. And He's overwhelmed me. He's made connections, illuminated verses, healed old wounds, and changed my perspective. But He's done so much more: He has revealed His love and sweetness to me in incredibly personal ways. I know more of Who He is. *That* is what satisfies! The answers, plans, and comfort come, too, but they come by getting to know the Doctor's heart.

Our fast-paced world doesn't encourage quiet time. There are a million voices clamoring for us to "do more" and "be more." Our own "to-do" lists are long and rarely see completion. We can easily believe that time with God is a luxury that robs us of the time we need for our "to-dos." In fact, *it prepares us*. Only God knows what our day holds. Time with Him prepares our minds and hearts for the future. It helps bring our will and plans in line with His.

This study was inspired primarily during my time in the mornings with God. I was "doing nothing" by the world's standards. True enough. *I* was doing nothing, but *He* was doing everything. I was just choosing to be open to His Word and quietly listen for His voice. And He was healing my wounded heart and mind. He was revealing His love to me, and preparing me for events and circumstances I had no idea were on the horizon. You will never be penalized for your time in the Doctor's "office." It is never "wasted time." That is a lie from the enemy. In fact, what you gain there will be the most precious treasure you will ever receive and the only thing on earth that can never be taken from you.

> Is anyone thirsty? Come and drink — even if you have no money! Come, take your choice of wine or milk — it's all free! Why spend your money on food that does not give you strength? Why pay for food that does you no good? Listen to me, and you will eat what is good. You will enjoy the finest food. Come to me with your ears wide open. Listen, and you will find life. (**Isaiah 55:1-3**)

taste and see

At the end of 2016, God kept bringing the word "intentional" to my mind. Everywhere I looked there it was. Due to my spiritual sickness at the time, which was actually much greater than my physical sickness, I immediately assumed that God meant I should be more intentional and disciplined in my areas of weakness. I had been freed from earning others' approval, but I still felt I had to earn His.

I purchased a jumbo planner and got to work. I made some goals and plans but nothing seemed to feel "right." I began to ask God some questions: "Will You show me your plan for *me*? Will You show me *my* purpose? What is Your direction for *me*?" I craved and begged for Him to give me clarity and received little.

One morning, I began to hear God say to me, "Seek *Me*." *I have been*, I thought. His response: "No. You're seeking plans and to-dos. Be intentional about seeking *Me*."

Suddenly, those "me" and "my" questions I'd been asking began to change. I began to simply ask God, "Will You show me more of Who *You* are?"

God began to lead me to begin praying these two Scriptures as I sat down to read the Bible each morning:

> … Speak, your servant is listening. (**1 Samuel 3:10**)

> If you are pleased with me, teach me your ways so I may know you and continue to find favor with you. (**Exodus 33:13 NIV**)

One morning, I picked up my Bible and the blinders began to drop. I began to see God for Who He really is. I can't explain it. It's something you simply have to experience for yourself.

Here's what I mean: Someone can put a piece of cheesecake in front of you. It can look delicious. Someone can tell you how amazing it tastes. But you are not *truly* going to believe how good it is until you taste it yourself. And what is the usual response when you taste something really amazing? You want more!

We can hear how amazing God is. We can know it in our heads. But we can't *truly* know God's goodness and love until we spend regular time with Him and in His Word and then *make choices* to know Him and trust Him in increasingly deeper ways. That is when we experience His goodness for ourselves — when we quit grasping for food that doesn't satisfy and begin to seek our satisfaction in Jesus.

Let's take a look at Matthew 4:1-11. It says *the Spirit* led Jesus into the wilderness. Why do you think that God sometimes leads us to seasons of feeling hungry, isolated, and vulnerable to enemy attack?

Satan tempts Jesus to satisfy His hunger in a number of ways. What does Jesus do in response each time (verses 4, 7 and 10)?

Why do you think it would have been wrong for Jesus to take Satan up on his offers?

What does Matthew 4:11 suggest about the power of quoting God's Word when we are being tempted?

How does this reflect James 4:7? The enemy attacks us repeatedly. We need to be armed and ready to speak truth back to him.

How is Jesus' hunger finally satisfied (verse 11)?

There is nothing wrong with being hungry. God created in us the hunger for love, purpose, and significance. We get into trouble when we try to feed on the wrong things to satisfy that hunger — performance, people, careers, appearance. The list is endless! But God created us to find our fulfillment *in Him*. When we do, we can more fully enjoy the people and blessings He gives us, because we aren't depending on them to make us feel significant and valuable. God is the only thing that can fill us up and satisfy us completely, yet still leaves us wanting more.

a heart healthy menu

God is not only our Doctor, but our Nutritionist. He knows exactly what diet plan will best meet our needs. His Word is always the main course.

Everyone's "meal" is going to be a little different, because God meets each of us so personally as we "dine" with Him. As we begin to "eat," He shows us how we can best connect with Him and feel His presence. He will show you how to personalize a menu that is right for the two of you. The following "menu" is a good basis for planning your feast time with God. It will likely change and evolve over time.

Simply start by resolving to eat regularly. We've all had many lies engrained in us throughout our lives. How did they become engrained? Through repetition. So doesn't it make sense that it would take repeatedly feasting on His truth to replace those lies?

appetizers

A feast always starts with an appetizer — a tasty morsel to tantalize our tastebuds and make us hungry for more. Spiritual appetizers (in the form of devotionals, worship music and taking time to express praise, love, and gratitude) makes us hungry for more of God. It sets the stage for the main meal.

These things can help us to open our hearts and focus our minds on Him:

- **Devotionals and Worship Songs.** On page 176, you'll find a list of devotional books, apps, and worship songs that can help to increase your hunger and connection with God.

- **Praise & Gratitude.** Thank God not only for what He's done, but *Who He is*. It's important to do this *especially* when we don't feel like it. It moves the focus from ourselves and our problems to God and His overwhelming goodness, power, and love.

main course

- **God's Word.** Food gives our physical bodies strength. But we have to actually consume the food in order to receive its benefits. And we can't eat just "once in a while." We have to eat quality food regularly or eventually we will get sick. Food doesn't just give us strength, it *is* our strength. Its nutrients sink deeply into our tissues and cells. It literally becomes part of who we are. The Word of God is our spiritual food. We have to consume it regularly in order for it to benefit us. As we do, it sinks deeply into our hearts and minds. His wisdom and strength become part of who we are.

Reading the Bible can feel intimidating and overwhelming at times. But *where* you start reading is not as important as *how* you approach His Word. When someone prepares a great meal for you, it reflects a loving heart. So approach God's Word as if it's a love letter. Because it is. It's God's love letter to you. He inspired men to write it so that we could know Him better — His ways and His heart. I often start my time in His Word with this simple prayer: "Lord, I'm here to seek You. Show me more of Who You are." He IS Love, friends. So it's not possible to know Him more deeply without experiencing His love for you. We need a deep sense of *Who God is* — not just information about Him. Without the Holy Spirit speaking to our open and willing hearts, Scripture is just words on a page.

In Exodus 33:18, Moses prayed that kind of prayer. He humbly, but boldly told God: "...show me your glorious presence."

How did God respond? (v.19) What "passed before" Moses?

Moses asked to see God and He showed Moses *His goodness*. That is the essence of who He is: *He is good.*

A delicious plate of food will never nourish you until you dig in! So, simply start reading somewhere, with an expectation to hear from a good and loving God, trusting He will lead you. If you are new to the Bible, or if you haven't been reading it regularly, the Gospels (Matthew, Mark, Luke, and John) are always a great place to start. Often, I will read a devotional (appetizer) and look up the Bible reference that goes along with it. I will read the entire chapter, not just the verse, so I understand the context. Often, I will then consult a Bible commentary. Since the Bible was originally written in Greek and Hebrew and during different times and cultures, commentaries offer information and background that bring greater insight and understanding into what the Bible writer was trying to communicate. My favorite commentary is called Enduring Word (enduringword.com). It is written in a clear, easy-to-read-and-digest format that doesn't require you to be a Bible scholar to understand.

Some of my favorite Bible translations are the New International Version (NIV), the New Living Translation (NLT) and The Voice (VOICE). They are written in plain language (without all the "thees" and "thous".) The Voice translation also has commentary and explanations peppered throughout the Scriptures which I have found very helpful. Biblegateway.com is an online Bible that provides dozens of translations for you to explore. Reading different translations of the same verses or passages can also help you to better understand Scripture.

- **Honest, Heartfelt Conversation.** As I wrote before, eating is social. Great meals often include great conversation. I have honest, heartfelt talks with God throughout my "meal." I ask Him questions as I'm reading His Word, tell Him about things I'm wrestling with, and specifically thank Him for how He is working in my life. Of course, I often bring Him various concerns and requests both for myself and others.

I keep a journal next to me as I read and pray. I write down insights He's giving me, as well as principles and verses I want to remember. I sometimes journal my prayers, too. This helps me to process what I'm learning. I can go back later and look at what I wrote so I can be reminded of what He's taught me. I've also found that writing what I'm learning helps "imprint" these lessons into my mind and heart.

Some of the most beautiful, honest, heartfelt prayers and insights are in the book of Psalms. David and the other writers of the Psalms were brutally honest with God, pouring out their whole hearts. They often expressed confusion and frustration with God's timing and ways. But here's what I noticed about these prayers: David and the other writers would express all their doubts and messiness, but then come back to verbalizing what they knew to be true. It usually sounds something like this (Melinda paraphrase!): "I'm surrounded and discouraged. I'm weary and broken. Where are You, God? I don't understand what You're doing! Yet I know You are good, loving, and faithful. I choose to trust You. Thank You for Who You are."

But I don't think David (and other psalmists) was directing his thoughts to God alone. I think he wrote the Psalms also *to remind himself* of the goodness and love of God, of how He had shown His faithfulness to David time and time again. When David was in deep, dark times, he encouraged himself with *remembering* that if God had been faithful in the past, He would be faithful in the future. He reminded himself of how much he was loved by God.

Prayer is an effective way of focusing on God and remembering Who He is. It's about sharing our hearts with God and asking Him to share His. As we get to know Him, we love Him more. And we want to please those we love. We start to care about the things they care about. I have seen many more answered prayers since I began to act on the truth of Psalm 37:4: "Take delight in the Lord, and he will give you your heart's desires."

As we delight in Him, *He* becomes the burning desire of our hearts — to know Him more, to pursue the things close to His heart. Those things are always for our ultimate good and His glory. He can give us our desires when they align with *His* heart and desires. And we are able to enjoy all the blessings He gives us more fully when we delight in Him — the Source of them. *He* is the gift. *He* is the whole enchilada, ladies.

Prayer isn't about wish fulfillment. It's about heart alignment.

dessert

When we start our day savoring God's goodness, it provides a sweetness and conversation that can last all day long. Every close relationship includes ongoing communication. It's vital to our relationship with God, because as we soon as we start our day, we are bombarded with many voices and messages, obligations, and struggles. We can easily become brainwashed. So much of what we encounter begins to challenge what we know to be true about God.

As I started to feel safer with God, I began to dialogue with Him more and more in the midst of my busyness and responsibilities. I'd pray, ask for His guidance, thank Him for His blessings (even the seemingly small ones), and tell Him what was on my heart. The more I focused on God throughout the day, intentionally drawing my focus and dependence onto Him, the less I feared. My joy, compassion, and confidence in Him grew by leaps and bounds.

Gradually, the Truth of Who He is — powerful, loving, able to do the impossible — and who I am in Him became my default position. My focus went to Him instead of to me. My mind shifted from thoughts like, *What am I doing wrong? Am I measuring up? I need to make things happen.* to thoughts like, *What could God be trying to tell or show me? God, can you help me? How do you want to use me in this situation? Thank You for helping me with that challenge.* It went from feeling like an awkward and forced hyperawareness to a more natural, ongoing dialogue. It will always take discipline for us to *stay* connected, but doesn't any relationship that's worth having?

God wants us in a place of humble dependence, *not* so He can oppress us, *but so He can set us free.* He longs for us to understand our need *for Him*, while never forgetting our position *in Him* as royalty. He will give us the power to lift up our weary heads, throw our shoulders back, and focus on His healing grace, power, and love.

> **Most of the time people want us dependent so they can take power from us. God wants us dependent so He can give power to us — *His*.**

How do you develop your own "language" with God? It can start with a simple prayer: "Lord, open my eyes to evidence of Your love for me."

Because God seemed so very scary to me, as I began to cautiously open my heart to Him, He began to speak through things that seemed "safe" to me. I'd be watching a favorite movie and suddenly feel like God was speaking very personally to me through the dialogue. Or, I'd be driving along listening to Chicago or Eric Carmen (I'm a huge fan of 80's music) and realize God was speaking through those lyrics directly to my heart. I'd ask God questions as I went about my day and suddenly see a sign or a bumper sticker that I immediately knew was God's answer to me. I know it sounds crazy. But a real, vibrant relationship with God often *does* seem crazy and difficult to explain. Because while God's message of love, salvation, and truth is the same for all of us, how He communicates it to each individual heart is unique to each of us.

While whole books have been written about how to hear God, I'll share with you a few simple methods God uses to speak to me:

- **Repetition.** Earlier in the study, I mentioned how in early 2017, I saw the word "intentional" so many times and in so many places I lost count. I knew God was trying to get my attention. I kept asking God what He was trying to tell me. It took some time, but eventually, I "heard" His voice in my head: "Be intentional about seeking Me."

- **Timing.** I'm on staff at my church. A few years back, I had the "feeling" that I should invite a certain ministry organization to come to our community. I was in my office, wondering if that was really God Who gave me that "feeling." *At that exact moment*, someone from that organization — who I had never met or even heard of — "randomly" called me and asked me if I'd be interested in bringing their organization to our church. *Timing!*

- **Consistent with God's ways with me.** I'm motivated and a hard worker, but my nature is to work methodically, which is another way of saying *slowly*. Ha! It takes me time to think through projects and develop them (case in point: God gave me the idea for this study almost four years ago!). It's just how I'm "wired." If I try to do too many things too quickly, I get overwhelmed, burn out, and shut down. So when an opportunity comes my way, I often ask myself, *Does considering this opportunity feel draining and overwhelming or does it feel challenging and energizing?* If it's from God, I've learned through experience that I feel energized — even if the opportunity feels challenging and scary. If I feel drained and overwhelmed by it, I've learned that it's a good indicator it's not the right time and/or opportunity for me personally. God challenges us, but He also honors how He's created and wired us.

- **Consistent with His Word.** Often times I get a feeling or thought about a situation or person. If those thoughts or "impressions" don't line up with God's Word or character, I know they are not from Him.

Earlier I suggested journaling your prayers and other thoughts as you read God's Word. I also recommend keeping a small journal or notebook in your purse or car so you can jot down insights and blessings God gives you throughout the day. It helps keep us connected and creates a record of God's goodness that we can look back on when we're struggling with fear, discouragement, and doubt.

There is no "formula" for hearing from God. It's like any relationship. The more you know and spend time with that person, the more you begin to know how they act and what they think. And like any habit, it takes time and practice. God has given our minds the beautiful ability to communicate and partner with Him, even as we perform our necessary daily tasks and activities.

> This is what Paul talks about it in **1 Thessalonians 5:16-18**: "Always be joyful. Never stop praying. Be thankful in all circumstances, for this is God's will for you who belong to Christ Jesus."

"Never stop praying" simply means an ongoing, constant, flowing communication with our Creator. Relationship and trust builds as we dialogue and partner with God in everything we do — every challenge, every decision, every victory — all day long. It's like having the best Doctor in the world on call 24/7. (But you never get a bill!)

The feast of His love, comfort, guidance, peace and so much more are always accesible to you.

Come to the table, friend. He's waiting to feed you.

your *heart* rewired

For most of my life, I was consuming a steady diet of lies. I knew the truth in my head, but it hadn't made its way into my heart. We make decisions based on what we know in our hearts. Unfortunately, I was often unknowingly making many decisions based on deceptions.

Some of the lies I listened to, I knew were lies, but I just couldn't seem to act on the truth. Some lies were comforting in a weird way. As long as I believed them, I could stay in "victim mode." I could more easily justify avoiding the hard choices.

The more we read God's Word and know His heart, the easier it will be for us to recognize lies. We'll be able to notice when they don't line up with the overwhelming love of God, Who He is, and what He says. When I'm unsure of the truth in a situation, I simply ask God, "Please help me to see the truth, Lord. Help me to see the person or circumstances through Your eyes."

I've also found this simple principle to be helpful in recognizing lies: Lies *starve*. Love *feeds*.

The lies the enemy whispers in our ears starve us of joy, peace, confidence, and freedom.

When we hear God's voice, it is the voice of love. His messages to us may challenge us at times and make us uncomfortable, but they never condemn us. His love feeds us. It makes us feel strong, secure, confident, bold, at peace.

Just like carpet becomes most worn in the pathways we use the most, our brains have pathways that become well worn by what we think about the most. They become our most natural way of thinking. And our thinking drives our behavior.

The beauty is that God designed our brains so that we can actually create new, healthy pathways to bypass those old, worn, harmful paths. We have the ability to retrain our brains to a new way of thinking. It takes time and repetition, but it *can* be done.

As I focused on God more and more, He began to show me how to replace the lies I'd believed with truth. He began to reveal beliefs I'd held that I didn't even realize were lies! But rather than just *thinking* a healthy thought to replace the lie in my head, I'd *speak the Truth out loud* as much as possible. At first, sometimes I did this literally *dozens* of times a day. This repetition is an important step in bringing the truth from head to heart.

changing your diet

Now let's explore where *your* heart needs to be rewired. Lies are overcome by replacing them with the truth of God's Word and *acting* on that truth. **Jesus shows us how to do this in Matthew 4:1-11.** In this passage, the enemy attempts to persuade Jesus to act in ways that were contrary to His Father's plan and purpose by twisting and distorting Scripture. The enemy is an expert at taking a little bit of truth and then warping it to try to discourage and deceive us. **Take a few minutes to read and meditate on those verses in Matthew.** Then, take some time to pray and ask God to reveal the lies that the enemy is using to poison *your* heart and mind.

In the "Now It's Your Turn" section below, write down those lies. For example, if you've written, "God only blesses me when I'm doing the right things" type "verses about God's love and grace" into a search engine. Choose a verse that refutes the lie. Then, write out the truth based on that Scripture and then the Scripture itself. Writing the truth helps imprint it on our minds and hearts. Saying the truth to yourself (both in your mind and out loud when you can) also helps to retrain your brain and way of thinking. **Some examples:**

Lie: I will always live in fear.

Truth: I can trust the One who died for me.

> "I prayed to the Lord, and he answered me. He freed me from all my fears." (**Psalm 34:4**)

Lie: I have to figure it all out.

Truth: God will show me the way one step at a time.

> "Your word is a lamp to guide my feet and a light for my path." (**Psalm 119:105**)

Lie: Results are all up to me.

Truth: Outcomes are not my job.

> "'Not by might nor by power, but by My Spirit,' says the Lord Almighty. (**Zech. 4:6 NIV**)

Lie: I will never have enough.

Truth: God will meet all my needs.

> "And my God will meet all your needs according to the riches of his glory in Christ Jesus." (**Phil. 4:19 NIV**)

Lie: It needs to happen now.

Truth: I can wait on God.

> "Wait patiently for the Lord. Be brave and courageous. Yes, wait patiently for the Lord." (**Psalm 27:14**)

Lie: I can't ever please God.

Truth: I am completely loved and accepted by God.

> "Yet now he has reconciled you to himself through the death of Christ in his physical body. As a result, he has brought you into

> his own presence, and you are holy and blameless as you stand before him without a single fault." **(Col. 1:22)**

The more I replaced lies with truth, the more peace and joy and freedom I felt. *New pathways slowly began to form.* Over and over throughout the day, I would bring my focus back to God and His love and truth until He began to be a part of nearly every thought in some way.

now it's *your* turn:

Lie:

Truth:

Scripture:

Lie:

Truth:

Scripture:

Lie:

Truth:

Scripture:

Lie:

Truth:

Scripture:

Lie:

Truth:

Scripture:

Repetition of truth is vital. Be intentional about making this a daily habit. Whatever we focus on becomes bigger in our minds and hearts. And we act on what we truly know in our hearts.

**Reject the Lie. Replace with Truth. Repeat often.
Continual life application results in gradual heart transformation.**

> *And may you have the power to understand, as all God's people should, how wide, how long, how high, and how deep his love is.*
> **(Ephesians 3:18)**

It was a familiar ritual. I'd done it for so long, it was difficult to remember what life was like before it. Each morning, often before I had even brushed my teeth, I went to my kitchen cabinet and took my first of three daily doses (handfuls) of health supplements. Trying desperately to beat back the pain and illness that plagued my body.

Actually, if I'm honest, I had a nagging sense of anxiety until I did this. I felt like any chance of improving my quality of life was dependent upon these supplements. I would experience great fear if I inadvertently missed a dose or run out of a supplement and couldn't replace it right away. They had become my life preservers — the things I clung to tightly for hope and security.

I'd been on many "protocols." But even when the protocol changed, I usually kept the supplements that I no longer took "just in case" I might need them again in the future. But in 2017 I was experiencing incredible encounters with the real Life Preserver — the real and living God. He had dramatically freed me from my old view of Him as a harsh and difficult taskmaster. He was empowering me to see Him with new eyes, to experience His love on a new level that I didn't even know existed. And as I did, I received spiritual healing that I didn't even know I needed. In addition, during the summer of 2017, I began to realize that I was beginning to receive the physical healing God had promised me years earlier.

I'm not saying this is always the case, but I recognized that for me, my spiritual and physical sickness were intertwined. As God began to peel back layers of spiritual toxicity in my mind and heart, my physical symptoms began to gradually improve. I was now drawing on the healing power of the real God, not the harsh god of performance and legalism that I had blindly served for so long. However, I still continued my daily ritual of taking my supplements.

a new Physician

But one evening, as I opened my kitchen cabinet, this thought popped into my head: *You don't need those anymore.* It took me by surprise (as God is prone to do). I thought, *What? I don't need those anymore?* But I already knew in my heart that I did not. And so, without another thought or even a trace of anxiety, I grabbed the kitchen trash can and began to throw away my old "life," one bottle at a time. God had given me permission to "let it go"! This was not a blind, impulsive act of faith. In fact, for the first time *my eyes were wide open.* I was only able to do this because God had opened my eyes to the fact that *He* was leading my health journey now.

The contents of these cabinets represented my old "Melinda-led" journey. I was on a new path now. I had to let go of my old "life preservers." I had embraced a new One — the God Who created my body and knew intimately exactly what I needed. My new Physician was someone who understood my complicated body and the complex physical problems that had stumped most healthcare professionals I had encountered. Over several months, God's overwhelming expressions of love for me had convinced me that my life was safe in His healing hands.

As I picked up and discarded each supplement, I felt a giddy sense of relief and freedom. Then I suddenly had a strong feeling that I should keep one supplement to represent each painful condition I had battled. These would be visual reminders so I would never forget all that He was delivering me from.

There were four other bottles that I felt uncertain about throwing away, so I set them aside until the end. I asked God to show me whether I should keep these or not. After some Google research, I noticed a common thread in three out of the four I had set aside: they had incredible *life-giving* properties. Although they had applications for a number of conditions, these were often used for vitality and energy and/or used to facilitate pregnancy or nourish a growing baby. God had been showing me over and over again the few weeks prior to this that He was giving me new life, so I knew I was to keep those three.

However, I couldn't seem to get any clarity as I prayed and researched the fourth supplement — Ox Bile (No, I'm not kidding!). Then I felt God say, "Don't look up 'Ox Bile.' Look up 'oxen.'" When I did, I found the description of oxen as animals that are often yoked with heavy loads. That had been me. Yoked by heavy loads of worry, fear, sickness, and performance. He was freeing me from all that. Ox Bile went into the garbage can with the rest of my old life.

a process of "letting go"

This was certainly not the first time God had clearly told me to "let it go." He had been preparing me for this moment for some time. Several years prior, I had hit a wall. Trying to fix, figure out, and control everything had left me confused, and bordering on despair. It was then that God cut through all the confusion and allowed me to see and experience the bright light of His love and grace.

Gently and patiently, He had told me to "let it go" when I had become burned out by trying to pursue my God-given writing and ministry dreams my way.

He assured me it was safe to "let go" of trying to fix or control when one of my precious children was making some heartbreaking choices.

He had been leading me to gradually let go of my chronically ill son into His hands.

In all these situations, I had to die to my way of doing things. When I finally did, God's life-giving love and power began to flow through me more freely. Gradually, new life began to sprout in my health, ministry, and relationships.

God, in effect, was saying, "Melinda, you don't know the future. You don't know your kids the way that I do. You don't know my plan for you and the gifts I've given you. Follow Me. One step at a time, I'll show you the way."

Read Matthew 4:18-22. What did Jesus say to Peter and Andrew? (v.19) What did they do? (v.20)

What did Jesus invite James and John to do? (v.21) How did they respond? (v.22)

Now let's look at Matthew 9:9. What did Jesus say to Matthew and how did he respond?

Do you see the pattern? Jesus invited them to follow Him. Without hesitation, these men immediately "let go" of their old lives and old ways of doing things and accepted His invitation. Coming face-to-face with the real and living God just seems to have that effect. Like me, they had to stay close to Jesus after they "let go." The new life was exciting, but unfamiliar. Without a Guide, they would fall back into old patterns.

Following is simple, but not always easy. Sometimes my "one-step-at-a-time" journey has seemed like a death march. Dying to self is painful. Allowing God to kill my ego, my agenda, and purge comfortable "saviors" is an excruciating process at times. Our human nature fights against it. But I find such comfort in this assurance:

> If you try to hang on to your life, you will lose it. But if you give up your life for my sake, you will save it. (**Matthew 16:25**)

Losing my life has saved me. All I had to do was let it go.

dying to be well

The Apostle Paul's conversion is a radical, inspiring example of the power of "letting go" of lies and embracing the love of Jesus. **Let's read about Paul's "aha" moment and what followed in Acts 9:1-20.**

Paul was a Pharisee, a member of a Jewish sect that strictly followed the Law of Moses. Paul did not believe in Jesus and considered his followers dangerous blasphemers. He didn't believe Jesus was Who He said He was. He didn't believe that He was the long-awaited Messiah Who died for our sins. Paul did everything he could to stamp out the message that Jesus was God. He was passionately committed to jailing and killing Christians. But Jesus loved Paul. God knew if Paul's passion was pointed in the right direction, He could use Paul in great ways. Jesus saw who Paul *could* be.

What question did Jesus ask Paul (then named Saul) in verse 4?

What was Paul's response (v.5)? Is this the response you would expect? Why or why not?

Paul immediately fell on the ground and closed his eyes. (v.4,8) When he opened them, what had happened?

What does it say he did for three days? (v.9)

Paul headed to Damascus on a passionate mission. But he met Jesus along the way. In an instant, Paul began to let go of all of his hatred and rigid ideas about Jesus and asked, "Who are you, lord?" (v.5) It's the most important question any of us can ever ask.

We can't know Who Jesus truly is until we are willing to open our minds and hearts and let go of our predetermined ideas about Who He is. It requires humility. Paul thought he knew it all, but he was spiritually blind. Jesus made him temporarily physically blind as well. This was a humbling experience. Instant blindness brought Paul to a place where Jesus had his full attention. He was literally blind to distractions.

For three days, verse 9 tells us that he didn't eat or drink. During these days, I can imagine Paul was rethinking so many things that he had once believed. He may have been mourning all the decisions and pain he had caused based on those lies. I believe God was using this time to "rewire" him. Paul was "dying" to his long-held ideas about God.

Who did Jesus send to Paul in verses 10-12? Jesus could have cured Paul without using this man. Why do you think He used a human to do this?

Look at verse 17. It says that Ananias "laid his hands on him" and called him "brother"? How do you think that would have made Paul feel?

By touching Paul and calling him his "brother," Ananias communicated God's love to Paul. This is remarkable because just a few days prior Paul was on a mission to kill men like Ananias. In fact, Ananias was initially terrified to go to Paul, but now he's calling him "brother"! He also said, "... Be filled with the Holy Spirit." (v.17) Paul's heart had changed during those three dark days. He was now ready to accept Jesus as His Savior and receive His Holy Spirit into His heart. He was now healed of both his physical and spiritual blindness.

After Ananias visited Paul, he did several important things in verses 18-20. First, he went to be baptized. He was well known for his hatred of Jesus. He now wanted to publicly identify as a follower of Jesus. Afterwards, he stayed with other followers of Jesus to be encouraged. Then, he "began preaching about Jesus." He couldn't keep quiet about the Source of the new life he had found.

What happened a short time later? (v.22-24)

When we begin to walk and speak in the truth, we can expect to be attacked. We may not encounter people who want to kill us, but we will likely experience people and circumstances that are designed to kill our message. Satan's greatest fear is that people will learn the truth about Who God is and His love and goodness. Paul experienced difficulties and attacks for the rest of his life. The only way that he was able to keep going was by depending on a loving, powerful God. Paul's life was hard. But God gave him this life-giving promise: "My grace is all you need. My power works best in weakness." (2 Corinthians 12:9) He gave Paul the power to continue one step at a time as he depended on Him.

the choice to let go

It comes down to this: Every patient has to be willing to surrender to their doctor. The patient can't be in control when the surgeon is doing his work. The patient has to trust that the doctor knows what he or she is doing. In order to be truly well, the patient has to let go of the old behaviors and mindsets that contributed to their sickness. Their "old self" has to die so they can be healthy, new, and whole.

On our faith journey, Jesus also calls us to die willingly. He doesn't force us. It's our choice. He invites us to die to our selfish desires, to our dreams, agendas, and plans. The enemy tries to convince us that it's suicide. In reality, as we choose to die to our way and ask God to lead us, we discover new life. We experience the freedom of being gently led, instead of being driven by our own ideas of success. Jesus is Living Water. When we empty ourselves of "us," there's room for Him to fill us with His purpose, His will, His power, and His dreams. And we will always be blessed by His loving presence in the journey.

The reason I so often struggled to believe that God was working for my good, is because I didn't truly believe that God *is* loving and good. I couldn't surrender my life to Him and embrace the truth of His love until I was willing to let go of the lies that I believed about Him. It's been a gradual process that is still ongoing.

Even as God changes our hearts, we will still struggle. We live in a world that is constantly trying to indoctrinate us. To get us to see things through a warped lens of lies and fear. Choosing to believe His love is true regardless of what we see or feel is not easy. It's not a one-time thing. It's a one-moment-at-a-time thing. It's the repetition of it doing it over and over again until it becomes our unconscious state, until it becomes our new default.

Our tendency is to focus on circumstances, obstacles, and feelings. Jesus gently challenges us to focus on *Him*. That doesn't mean our emotions and circumstances aren't real. It isn't denying reality. It's simply acknowledging that a bigger, more powerful, loving Reality is right there in front of us. And as we focus on Him, He will give us everything we need to walk through all of life's obstacles and jumbled emotions. We aren't alone. A God who loves us more than we can imagine has already made a way for us through whatever we face. We don't have to figure it out. We just have to focus and follow. We can surrender to His love.

Your life is never safer than when it's placed in the hands of the One who gave His life to save it.

your *heart* rewired

In the last "Your Heart Rewired" section, you wrote lies you believed, and truths from God's Word that refuted those lies. Now, here's the "secret ingredient" to experiencing the beauty of those truths: They are just words if we don't understand that they come from a heart of love. We will be able to internalize and embrace the truth much more easily and passionately when we view it through the lens of God's overwhelming love for us.

This week, I'd like to challenge you to ask God to give you eyes to see, and ears to hear evidence of His love for you as you go about your day. Maybe it's an unexpected phone call from a friend, or a song on the radio that you know is speaking directly to you. Not only will you feel His love, you'll also begin to recognize how God speaks and encourages you very personally and uniquely.

The writer Luke starts his book of the Bible by writing how he, along with others, had seen *with their own eyes* the miracles and love of Jesus. What they witnessed was so amazing, they had to write it down. They had to share their "eyewitness reports" with others: "Many people have set out to write accounts about the events that have been fulfilled among us. They used the eyewitness reports circulating among us from the early disciples. (**Luke 1:1-2**)

I challenge you to begin to write down a few "eyewitness reports" of God's goodness that you have experienced recently (see next page). Also, consider keeping a small notebook with you throughout the day so you can keep an ongoing record of "eyewitness reports." They are great reminders of God's love and activity when we are feeling alone or discouraged.

Continual life application results in gradual heart transformation.

my recent "eyewitness reports":

> *Seek his will in all you do,*
> *and he will show you*
> *which path to take.*
> **(Proverbs 3:6)**

As we walk through life's broken journey of hurts, struggles, and uncertainties, the path ahead can seem impossibly scary. We feel paralyzed. At times, we believe we lack the courage to keep moving forward. We look for solid ground, but only see nothingness. We only see the chasm that lies between where we are and our deliverance.

God lovingly whispers to us to change our focus. He tells us, "You can trust the One who died for you. You must believe. Not in your sufficiency, but in Mine." The love *of* and *for* our Father, our Physician, will give us the courage to move past our fear.

Changing our focus — from our circumstances, our performance, or our future — to our Physician is what will allow us to rest. Jesus never promised an easy journey, but He did promise to never leave us. He walks us patiently through each and every step.

> Never will I leave you; never will I forsake you. (**Heb. 13:5 NIV**)

God doesn't tell us all the answers, but He already knows them and just how to lead us. He never withholds instruction from those who are willing to learn. He sees mistakes and disobedience as teaching moments, and opportunities for His children to grow.

He understands that certain tasks can seem particularly overwhelming and scary to us. Making hard choices. Doing something new, or something that seems beyond our abilities. Living with hard circumstances that have no end in sight.

This is what a gentle Jesus keeps telling me: "Follow Me. *Today. This moment.* Let's concentrate on what I've asked you to do *right now*. Focus on following, not *performing*. Not your circumstances. Don't focus on tomorrow. I'm already there. I have the answer. I'll meet you when you get there and give you what you need."

When I remember that, instead of fearful, I feel fierce. *Bold.* Because I know that the outcome and the journey is led by someone far wiser, stronger, and more capable than I am. Someone who loved me enough to die for me — even though I didn't do a single thing to be worthy of it.

I don't always understand what God is doing in my journey. At times, God and I have had some heated discussions. But here is a choice I have to make over and over: To *trust* Him. I find myself saying it throughout the day, "I choose to trust You, Jesus." If I trust the One who is leading my journey, I don't have to know the future. I don't have to understand His ways. I only have to follow His leading.

Following is just taking the next step, trusting that, one step at a time, He will provide solid ground underneath our shaky feet.

changing our view of healing

I've always assumed that when Jesus healed people in the Bible, it was in an instant. One moment, they are blind. The next they can see. They are paralyzed. Suddenly, they can walk. Boom. *Healed.* Happily ever after. The End. Mic drop. Cue the credits.

As someone who has received divine and powerful healing — in heart, mind, and body — I can tell you a sobering, yet freeing truth I've discovered during this healing journey.

Healing isn't a moment that happens to you. It's a truth that you walk out, allowing God to work through you.

Isaiah tells us that "by his wounds we are healed." (Isaiah 53:5 NIV) Healing is freedom. The truth is that when we accept Christ's payment on the cross for our sins, *we are healed*. We are free. Free from bondage to our impulses, emotions, and desires. Free from having to earn our worth or salvation. Free from having to figure it all out. Free from trying to have to heal ourselves.

But continually walking out all aspects of healing truth is far more difficult than I anticipated. This was new territory for me. I knew how to walk in bondage. I knew how to walk like a sick person. As much as I hated the chains, I found some strange comfort in their familiarity. I didn't know what it looked like to walk as a healed, free woman.

Even though I am free, the enemy continually tries to convince me I'm still in prison. What's the cure? *Focus*. Choosing to turn my focus to God and make choices that reflect I am free — even when I don't *feel* free. It's a journey I will be on for the rest of my life. Sometimes I stumble. But that's okay: I have the best Physician.

movement is medicine

Two examples of healing in the gospels provide some powerful insights into what walking in our healing looks like.

In Luke 17, Jesus heals 10 men with leprosy: a horrible, contagious, incurable disease. Lepers were isolated from the general population. The impact on their hearts, minds, and bodies can't be overstated. They were literally *dead men walking*.

> As he entered a village there, ten men with leprosy stood at a distance, crying out, "Jesus, Master, have mercy on us!" He looked at them and said, "Go show yourselves to the priests." And as they went, they were cleansed of their leprosy. (**Luke 17:12-14**)

In Week Three, we looked at the healing of the crippled man at the pool of Bethesda. If you remember, Jesus told him to "Stand up, pick up your mat, and walk!" (John 5:8) At the moment Jesus spoke those words, a healing energy coursed through the man and returned life to his limbs. He stood and walked *for the first time in 38 years*.

Here are few of the truths that these two passages teach us:

- **Healing isn't passive.** It requires action. Not the action of *earning*. The action of *receiving*.

   Jesus told the 10 lepers to start walking to the priests. He told the paralyzed man to pick up his mat and walk. They were healed the moment Jesus spoke it. But it was *their choice* to act upon what they were given.

   The jail cell can be open, but we aren't free until we walk through the door. We can be well, but the healing isn't enjoyed until we walk out of the hospital.

- **The Healer is always within reach.** Hundreds of sick and dying people are waiting at the pool of Bethesda, waiting to be healed. *And the Healer is right there. Right there!* Standing right in their midst. They just don't recognize Him. Don't we all tend to reach for false saviors even when *the* Healer is *right there*?

   When we direct our prayers toward Him, He reminds us of the Truth: *You are healed. You are free. Now stand up and walk like it, Princess. I'm walking right beside you, holding your hand.*

- **Healing transcends what we see or feel.** There are moments and days when I don't feel healed. My mind and body sometimes responds in pain to the memories of old traumas. Sometimes I'm under spiritual attack. Other times, I don't understand *at all* why I am in pain. I just know God told me He is healing me. And that is true no matter how I feel. I still struggle, but I am not who I was. At times, my mind and heart are overcome with feelings of fear, discouragement, and doubt. I just have to take the word of the Healer. Feelings are real, but they aren't aren't truth. *He is.* He is always faithful to His promises.

Luke tells us that the ten lepers were cleansed "as they went." When they first started walking, they didn't *feel* healed. They didn't *look* healed. They just had the promise that it was so. Each step was a step empowered by faith, believing that their healing was real even though they couldn't feel it or see it yet.

After 38 years of paralysis, I imagine there may have been days when the man at Bethesda woke up with a twinge of doubt that his healing was *really* real. Every step he took was a deliberate act of faith that what Jesus spoke over him was true.

No matter what our circumstances tell us, no matter how we feel, we are healed. We are free. As we focus on the Healer, He gives us the power to live in the truth. Each of our healing journeys is going to look different because our wounds are different. The barriers in our hearts and minds are different. Our Healer's purpose for each of our journeys is different.

The common thread, however, is that we have an enemy who tells us we are forever in bondage to our wounds. He can't change the truth of our freedom, so he tries to get us to doubt it.

As we choose to walk in the truth, he begins to lose his power over us. As we choose to rise above our feelings, they gradually fall in line with the truth.

walk while we're waiting

Until we're in heaven, our sin nature will prevent us from *fully* experiencing the mind, heart, and body healing we were given at the cross. As we wait, Jesus left us with His Holy Spirit to energize and comfort us, remind us of truth, and give us power as we make choices to walk in freedom step by step. To keep moving forward when the journey seems all uphill. It isn't easy. But the more we exercise the muscle of walking in the Truth, the more natural it will become.

The healing journey can feel kind of like climbing a mountain. It takes energy and effort. But one step at a time, you keep making progress and going higher. Then, suddenly, your foot slips and you begin to slide. You have to stop and refocus and become more intentional in your journey. Gradually, you become stronger. Those slips become less frequent. You're able to stop more quickly, so you don't fall as far. It doesn't take you as long to regain lost ground. You keep moving higher, even if it's not as quickly as you may like.

When I first started on this healing journey, I was sure that my days of pain were behind me. It was a straight shot to the mountain top, baby! I believed that my physical struggles and my battles with anxiety, people-pleasing, and discouragement were a distant memory. But they *weren't*. And they *aren't*.

As God brings physical, emotional, and spiritual toxins to the surface, I feel pain. To cope, I sometimes find myself going back to old ways of managing stress and problems. Or, I get busy and distracted and find myself forgetting that I don't have to perform for God or anyone else. But guess what? I don't stay in those places as long as I used to. I recognize the warning signs of my descent a lot sooner. I reach for the Healer a lot quicker. And He repeatedly assures me that while I still have ups and downs, I'm trending upward. My lows aren't as low. And my highs keep getting higher. As I keep climbing, I get closer to Him. And the truth sinks in more deeply: How very much my Father loves me. And as I shift my focus from my fall to my Father, the truth reminds me that I am free.

I don't know what the road ahead looks like. There are days the journey seems especially painful. Some days, I struggle with feeling decidedly *not healed*. But like the man at Bethesda, or the lepers on their way to the priest, I know what my Healer told me. I cling to the truth that God *has* healed me, He *is* healing me and He *will* heal me.

I'll just have to walk and see. One intentional step of faith at a time.

Doubt can only cripple us if we stop walking.

your *heart* rewired

> Do not merely listen to the word, and so deceive yourselves. Do what it says. Anyone who listens to the word but does not do what it says is like someone who looks at his face in a mirror and, after looking at himself, goes away and immediately forgets what he looks like. But whoever looks intently into the perfect law that gives freedom, and continues in it — not forgetting what they have heard, but doing it — they will be blessed in what they do. (**James 1:22-25 NIV**)

Reading, knowing, and memorizing Scripture is very important. But unless we put what God says into action, it's only head knowledge. *Action* is what brings what we know in our heads into our hearts. When we act on what God says is true, we see Him work in our lives. Our trust in Him grows. His love and faithfulness is not something we just know in our heads. We've *experienced* it. We now know it in our hearts. That is powerful! Satan wants to keep you in a place of head knowledge. He knows that when you begin to take God at His Word, and act on what He tells you, you will see how truly amazing, sweet, and trustworthy God is. While God may not always act or respond in the method or timing we would like, we will still experience His love in the midst of our confusion and struggles. We know He is *for* us. We just won't believe Satan's lies anymore! We are now building on a firm foundation of truth.

> I will show you what it's like when someone comes to me, listens to my teaching, and then follows it. It is like a person building a house who digs deep and lays the foundation on solid rock. When the floodwaters rise and break against that house, it stands firm because it is well built. (**Luke 6:47-48**)

Look back at page 137. Take the Truths you are trying to believe and write one way you can act on each.

See the example on the next page to help guide you.

Example:

Truth: God will never leave me (see Deut. 31:6). I can trust Him to direct me one step at a time (see Proverbs 3:5-6).

Action: When I find myself getting anxious and trying to figure everything out on my own, I will ask God to show me the next step He wants me to take. Even if that step seems difficult, scary, or crazy, I will take it, knowing God sees the big picture and is right beside me.

Truth:

Action:

Truth:

Action:

Truth:

Action:

Continual life application results in gradual heart transformation.

> *Yet I still dare to hope when I remember this: The faithful love of the Lord never ends! His mercies never cease. Great is his faithfulness; his mercies begin afresh each morning.*
> **(Lamentations 3:21-23)**

Every day, I talk to and spend time with Jesus. As I do, I fall in love. I just know He is "the One." The One who I can trust with all my heart. I feel safe. I know I have nothing to fear with Him beside me. I feel joy, peace, and rest.

Then I go about my day and I slowly drift toward memory loss. I find that His voice gets harder to hear amidst clamoring voices and challenging people. I receive message after message that tells me I can't rest. That I have to do it all on my own. That I have to do more, be more. That I'm not safe.

Past traumas and events also dim my awareness and ability to embrace the Love that is right in front of me. The Love that will never leave me.

stuck on repeat

Our past experiences and beliefs get stored into our long-term memory. Often-repeated lies, traumas, chronic pain, and difficulties become firmly implanted in our minds and hearts. We can even get stuck in an unhealthy focus on *good* things of the past — the "glory days." And, sadly, it prevents us from seeing and experiencing the "new thing" that God desires to do in and through us.

Old memories are well-engrained, like those well-worn paths of carpet in our homes. New experiences and reminders of His love are there, but we often go back to those old paths — old beliefs, experiences, and hurts. Those old paths may not always be healthy, but they are familiar. At least we know what to expect.

We often have more experience with our past life than the new life of truth, love, and healing that Jesus offers us. It's easier and safer to remember the pain and the lies rather than embrace a love that we don't quite trust yet. Or, sometimes we focus on the past because it seems better than the present or the future.

Either way, it keeps us from moving forward. We have to repeatedly and intentionally train our minds to focus on the One who is always doing a "new thing" in us and in our circumstances. When we focus on the past, we not only miss the new thing, but we miss *Him* in the journey. That is the real tragedy.

As we've talked about throughout this study, it takes time after time of remembering and acting on His love to drive it from our short-term consciousness to our long-term memory banks. As we do, our memory of Him and His love gets easier to accept and embrace. We remember the past, but we're no longer stuck in it.

Pursuing relationship with Jesus is an invitation, not a command. He doesn't *demand* that you love and spend time with Him. He wants it to be our choice. He lovingly says, "I'm here. My love for you is always available. I want a deep and continual relationship with you. I died so we could have one. Will you join Me, Daughter?"

focus is a choice — over and over again

The Creator of the universe wants a personal relationship with us. He is standing right there in front of us. But social media or 1,000 other things seem more interesting. That's only true because we often don't choose to focus on Him long enough for our barriers to come down, allowing us to experience His love and see Him for Who He truly is.

Our relationship with God is a love story. But it takes time to remove the heart barriers between us. Think about it. At the start of any relationship, you feel stressed and nervous. You're not quite sure if you'll be accepted. You bring old baggage into your time together. You focus mostly on yourself and your performance. But gradually, as you spend time together and begin to feel safe, your focus shifts to the other person. You start to let your guard down. You slowly begin to feel safe enough to honestly share your heart. You begin to let go of your apprehension and self-focus long enough to relax and really hear the other person.

It's the same in our relationship with Jesus. As we spend time with Him each day, focusing on getting to know Him and experiencing His sweetness, we can't help but sense His love. The more we focus on Him, other distractions seem less enticing. Our problems seem less overwhelming. His compelling, captivating love just flat out wins our hearts. We come to Him exactly as we are, but His love motivates us to let go of those attitudes and habits that come between us.

Suddenly, we view our past, present, and future through a different lens. He opens our eyes to His sweetness, patience, and care for us, through our past traumas, mistakes, and confusion. We gain confidence in His ability, willingness, and power to care for us today and tomorrow.

God created our minds and hearts with the incredible ability to renew and heal themselves. What a gift! But it's just that. *A gift.* He offers it. It's up to us to receive and use the gift. As we make intentional choices to do so, our hearts and minds are renewed.

Renewal comes through repetition.

We can't walk on the treadmill once in a while and expect our hearts to be in tip-top shape forever. Likewise, we can't choose to think positive, God-centered thoughts now and then and expect that our minds will never experience negativity again.

Even once our hearts and minds do get to a healthier place, we can't quit being intentional in our choices. If we do, we'll quickly find ourselves sick again. Even the best athlete in the world will lose their edge and endurance if he or she doesn't continue to exercise and eat a healthy diet. They will never "arrive" at a place where it's no longer necessary. Neither will we — not on this side of heaven.

I'll say it again: *Renewal comes through repetition*.

Let's take a moment to look at what Paul says in **Romans 12:1-2**:

> And so, dear brothers and sisters, I plead with you to give your bodies to God because of all he has done for you. Let them be a living and holy sacrifice — the kind he will find acceptable. This is truly the way to worship him. Don't copy the behavior and customs of this world, but let God transform you into a new person by changing the way you think. Then you will learn to know God's will for you, which is good and pleasing and perfect.

Write some of the mercies of God that you have experienced just this week:

What mercies do you think Paul may have been referring to in verse 1? How has God shown us mercy?

What is the greatest evidence He has ever given us of His mercy?

When are you most likely to forget God's mercies to you? What helps you to remember?

What do you think Paul meant when he says to "give your bodies to God because of all he has done for you. Let them be a living and holy sacrifice . . ." (v.1)? Was he referring only to the physical body?

Why do you think Paul would focus his readers on God's mercies immediately before He urged them to "be a living and holy sacrifice"?

What Paul is saying is this: Remembering and being aware of God's love fuels action. It prompts us to want to please Him and focus on Him more and more. The more we focus on Him, the more we experience all that He has to offer: Peace, Joy, Love . . . and so much more. Because He *is* all those things. We can't get closer to Him without experiencing them.

In other words, we have to make a *choice* to focus. God doesn't *make* us focus on Him. Paul says "offer." It's an act of our will. It comes before the transformation of the mind.

Romans 12:1-2 can be summed up in three points:

1. **Remember God's mercies and how much He has done.** You didn't earn them, but considering how amazing that love is, doesn't it seem reasonable to want to love and serve Him?

2. **Choose to offer your whole self as a living sacrifice.** Paul experienced sickness, beatings, shipwrecks, prison, and persecution throughout his journey. He knew better than most what a great cost was involved in following Christ. If he can joyfully and wholeheartedly "urge" us to do the same, that love must be pretty captivating.

3. **As you do numbers 1 and 2 consistently and repeatedly, this will be the result:** You will be gradually transformed by the renewing of your mind.

I'll say it again: *Renewal comes through repetition.*

The more we renew our minds by focusing on God, the more we are transformed. Transformation is a gradual process. It's a choice we have to make *over and over* again. To remember His love, to focus on Him and His love, and to gradually be transformed. The more we do it, the more it becomes engrained in us. It will never be easy to maintain our focus, because we are so easily distracted, but it becomes more natural.

Now let's look at Deuteronomy 7:22. In the last chapter, we talked about how God promised the Israelites a new land, a new home. He led them out of their slavery in Egypt and promised them freedom in a land all their own. But they were too stubborn and unbelieving to possess it. So they wandered in the wilderness for 40 years while the Promised Land was right there for the taking.

By Deuteronomy 7, most of those who had traveled out of Egypt have died. Their children and grandchildren will possess the land instead. God had to bring the Israelites to a point where they were willing to give their whole hearts to Him. Not because He's a control-freak taskmaster, but because He knew that depending on Him was the only way they were ever going to make it to the Promised Land. It was impossible to do on their own strength and wisdom. They had to choose to do it His way before they would see all the benefits the Promised Land had to offer.

God works the same way with us. I had to finally say, "I can't do it my way anymore, God." And He said, "Finally, Daughter, now I can show you the Promised Land." But the Promised Land is entered little by little. God wants us to gain a deeper understanding of Him, His love, His power, and His goodness, as we take steps into the Promised Land. If He gave us all His wisdom and benefits at once, we might focus on the Promised Land itself instead of Him. We'd depend on circumstances and the gifts of God, instead of God Himself. And we'd soon find ourselves in the wilderness again.

> Deuteronomy 7:21-22 (NIV) illustrates this concept: "Do not be terrified by them, for the Lord your God, who is among you, is a great and awesome God. The Lord your God will drive out those nations before you, little by little. You will not be allowed to eliminate them all at once, or the wild animals will multiply around you."

God promises all of us complete access to His love, mercy, grace, goodness, kindness, and so much more. He may at times give us assurance through His Holy Spirit that He is going to do something very specific in our lives and situations. But usually the details and timing are vague. It rarely unfolds as quickly as we would like or the way we imagine.

How have you seen God work in your life little by little? How have you benefited from His *gradual* work in your life?

Let's go back to Deuteronomy 7:22: "You will not be allowed to eliminate them all at once, or the wild animals will multiply around you."

Every battle makes us stronger and prepares us for the next one. If God transformed us all at once, we wouldn't learn the lessons along the way that gradually make us stronger. We wouldn't be adequately prepared for the battles we will continue to experience until we one day meet Him face-to-face.

Finally, when we begin to let go of old habits, it takes time to form new healthier, God-centered habits. If God magically removed our desire for them overnight, we would likely just fill those empty spaces with something even more dangerous to our fragile and fickle hearts and minds.

Look at how much repetition there is in the Bible! The New Testament books of Matthew, Mark, Luke and John? They're basically the same story told in four different ways. God tells us 365 times in the Bible not to fear. He repeated the same things over and over again to His disciples. Was it because God ran out of things to say? *Ummm... no.* It's because He knows that we are forgetful creatures. And when we forget Him and His love, we are like sheep who go astray. And we can find ourselves in very dangerous places.

He wants His Word, His promises, and His love to go down deep. He wants it to transform how we live, how we think, and how we approach Him. He desires deep relationship with us. But no deep relationship is developed overnight. And it can never be placed on auto-pilot.

I'll say it again: Renewal comes through repetition.

leaving the past behind

The Israelites struggled to leave the past behind, too. **Read Exodus 15:22-27.**

In Exodus 14, God has just led the Israelites out of slavery in Egypt. He split the Red Sea so they could walk across and escape the Egyptians. He just *split the Red Sea*! Let that sink in. Now, just *days later*, what did the Israelites do in Exodus 15:23?

Okay, bearing that in mind, **read Exodus 16**. At the end of Exodus 15 (v.24-27), God had miraculously provided water for them in the desert. So, let's take a moment for a brief recap: In the course of a few days, God freed them from slavery, split the Red Sea and provided water in the desert. So now they *really, really* trust Him, right? What does it say the Israelites are doing in Exodus 16:3?

That's right! Complaining again. They want to go back to Egypt! They long to go back to *slavery*! I used to be so rough on the Israelites. I'd think, *How could they think like that, after all God had just done for them?* Until I realized that I'm just as forgetful.

Like Israel, I have been conditioned by many years of trauma and struggle. I grew up with a view of God as a detached taskmaster who was driving me to perform. I believed nothing I did would ever satisfy Him. Combined with 20 years of chronic pain, and a lifetime of heart-wrenching family struggles, I felt enslaved. Enslaved to God's demands. Enslaved to circumstances. Enslaved to disappointment. Enslaved to fear.

In 2017, as I wrote earlier, God began to open my eyes to Who He really is. I was finally ready to see Him. I realized that He is not a taskmaster. He is a loving Father. Because I accepted Jesus as my Savior, He sees me as He does His own Son! He paid the price for my sin on the cross, so I don't have to perform. Whatever I "do" for Him should come from a place of grateful love, not fear or obligation.

As He healed my view of Him, and I experienced His love, gradually my body and emotions began to follow. I began to feel free from old mindsets, and physical, and emotional pain. None of those things completely disappeared, but I could feel their hold on me gradually loosening. I thought I was on easy street!

And then I started to face obstacles again. I began to think, *Was all that really real? Is God really healing me? I didn't think it would look like this.* And gradually, I began to go back to a "slave mentality." I started to manage my expectations. I began to rely on old "masters" — diets, supplements — to make me feel better or distract me. I slowly slipped back to old mindsets and my pain began to increase, both physically and emotionally.

Even though the path of pain and brokenness was horrible, it was familiar. I knew what to expect. A new path of healing and freedom was unpredictable. I had to completely rely on God because I had no idea what my healing path looked like. And I wasn't sure if I entirely trusted Him yet. Walking in healing was hopeful. And hope is scary. It can feel dangerous. Because if it is *false* hope then we are going to be crushed. Better to not hope at all. The enemy wants us to think that the hope God offers is false hope. That when we hit obstacles, it means that He has forsaken us. That God has misled us. And those are lies!

Freedom is wonderful. But *walking in freedom* isn't easy. It won't always look like we expect it to look. We will encounter obstacles and circumstances that don't make sense. We have to totally rely on the only One who knows our healing path — because it's going to look different for each of us.

Walking in freedom isn't *passive*. It's a continual choice to think and act in ways that reflect the freedom we've been given. To not "go back to Egypt." To trust that the "new thing" that God did in our hearts and minds is really real.

In what ways and areas do you "go back to Egypt" in your own life?

What behaviors/thoughts characterize those times?

What is the result when you do those things? What are the consequences for you personally?

The Israelites had been slaves in Egypt for 400 years. The people who walked out of Egypt had never known what it was like to be free. A slave mentality was engrained in Israel through repetition. After many years of lies and bondage, thinking like slaves seemed normal to them. God gave them freedom and wanted them to think a new way. How? *Through repetition.* He wanted thinking about Him and trusting Him to become their new normal. How? *Through repetition.*

When we associate a person, memory, or activity with pain and disappointment, it takes many good experiences to rewire us. Our human inclination is to stifle pain when it surfaces. Instead, God wants us to see it as an opportunity for Him to comfort us and bring a deeper level of healing. As He does, we begin to associate His comfort with that person or memory instead of the pain. He is a gentle Healer.

Read Deuteronomy 11:18-20 (NIV): "Fix these words of mine in your hearts and minds; tie them as symbols on your hands and bind them on your foreheads. Teach them to your children, talking about them when you sit at home and when you walk along the road, when you lie down and when you get up."

Let's go back to Exodus 16. Re-read verses 7-20. Why do you think that God wouldn't allow them to gather more manna than they needed for each day?

Why did some of the people disobey God and try to "hoard" more than their daily share?

What things do you do to make yourself feel more secure about the future?

Are these things that lead you closer to God or further away? Why?

Israel didn't leave the past behind. They kept going back to Egypt — not physically, but in their minds. "Oh, we'd be better off in Egypt." They saw themselves as victims. They were easily led like the slaves they *used to be*, instead of choosing to believe what God said was true and following Him no matter what their feelings and circumstances were telling them.

Belief is a *choice*. Choosing to act like what God said is true even when we can't see it. If we don't replace the things we leave behind with a choice to focus on and trust God — over and over again —we will just replace them with another idol that will enslave us. When Israel refused to believe and trust God, they left their old master (Egypt) and began to embrace new gods.

We will always be mastered by someone or something. It's our choice as to who or what that is going to be. Will it be something that will let us down and fail us and perhaps destroy us? Or, will it be our Creator who loves us so much and only wants to lead us to the Promised Land? God loves you — no matter what. Our focus on the Father is fickle. His focus on us never fails.

Even when our minds forget what our hearts know, His love for us remains unchanged. Every morning and throughout the day, He sends reminders of why you fell in love with Him in the first place. Those are the "God sightings" we talked about in Week Seven. God's love never fades and never fails, even when our memory of it does. In gentle tones, and in words that are personal to each of us, Jesus whispers: *My love is true. My promises can be trusted. You just need to act on them. As you act on them, what you know in your mind becomes embedded in your heart. Focus on Me. It will remind you of My love.*

A deep sense of the love of the Father changes everything. His presence beckons us to live in the present. Trauma is cumulative, but *so is healing*. As you focus on Him and take one step, one choice at a time, the Great Physician breathes new life into you. Don't give up on the Treatment. He will never give up on you.

Now go, my beautiful friend, walk in the freedom of a whole new you.

> You will keep in perfect peace all who trust in you, all whose thoughts are fixed on you! (**Isaiah 26:3**)

where do I go now?

- **Revisit Chapter 6** and start eating from the "Heart Healthy Menu" daily.

- **Look for the** *Rewired Heart* **devotional.** It's coming soon on Amazon! This interactive devotional will help you continue to put into practice the principles of REST.

- **Visit my website** at **newthingcreations.com/rewired-heart-printables** for free artwork and printables that will encourage you on your journey and remind you of the truths God has been teaching you.

resources

While there are many amazing devotionals, musicians and commentaries out there, the following is a brief list of some of the ones I personally read, listen to, and use often. Ask God to lead you to the ones (these and/or others) that are right for you.

Devotionals

Streams in the Desert by L.B. Cowman and James Reimann (Grand Rapids: Zondervan, Revised Edition, 1999)

Jesus Calling: Enjoying Peace in His Presence by Sarah Young (Nashville: Thomas Nelson, 2004)

Jesus Today: Experience Hope in His Presence by Sarah Young (Nashville: Thomas Nelson, 2012)

Jesus Always: Embracing Joy in His Presence by Sarah Young (Nashville: Thomas Nelson, 2016)

You Version – The Bible App (https://www.youversion.com/the-bible-app/)

My Utmost for His Highest, Updated Language edition by Oswald Chambers and James Reimann, ed. (Grand Rapids: Our Daily Bread Publishing, 2017)

Worship Music Artists

Keith Green

Rich Mullins

Matthew West

Chris Tomlin

Third Day

MercyMe

Casting Crowns

Audrey Assaud

Darlene Zschech

Bible Study Commentaries/Sermons/Aids

Enduring Word (http://enduringword.com)

Bible Gateway (http://biblegateway.com)

The Spurgeon Center for Biblical Preaching at Midwestern Seminary (https://www.spurgeon.org/resource-library/)

about the author

Melinda Means is a woman who was radically changed when the God she *thought* she knew since childhood opened her eyes to the overwhelming depth of His love for her. She loves speaking, writing, and pointing women to the Father so they can experience *for themselves* the healing power of His incredible, captivating love.

She is the author of *Invisible Wounds: Hope While You're Hurting* and co-author of *Unraveled Roots: Exposing the Hidden Causes of Damaging Behaviors* (2020) and *Mothering From Scratch: Finding the Best Parenting Style for You and Your Family* (Bethany House, 2015). Melinda is also an artist, Certified Professional Life Coach, and is currently pursuing her master's in Clinical Christian Counseling. She is on staff at her church, wife to Mike and mom to two very entertaining young adult children.

You can visit her website at **newthingcreations.com**. You can find her on Instagram at **instagram.com/newthingcreations**. Reach her via email at **newthingcreations@gmail.com**.

acknowledgements

To my husband, Mike, I owe a huge debt of gratitude for reading version after version of this book and painstakingly helped me to edit it. He was unflinchingly honest, yet gentle, in his critiques and encouraging every step of the way. He is always my biggest cheerleader and believes in me even when I sometimes don't believe in myself. He didn't just edit *Rewired Heart* with me. He took the journey with me and supports me as I try to live it out in messy, very imperfect ways. I love you to the moon and back.

To Freda, my big sister, who listened to me talk about this project for months and patiently gave encouragement and feedback while I read chunks of this manuscript as we took a cross country road trip. Your "little" sister still looks up to you and your words of support and encouragement meant more than I can express. Much love to you, sis.

To Bonita, my very dear friend and sister from another mister. This incredible woman was a huge encouragement as I struggled to get my thoughts from my heart to the page. God used and uses her often to encourage and challenge me in my ongoing "rewiring" process. She believed in me and this message and told me so often. I love you dearly.

A heartfelt "thank you" to my Rewired buddies: Haley, Jessica, Angie, Sheila, Kerry, Susan, Julia, Tina, and Judy. These amazing women took this *Rewired Heart* journey with me when it was in its "raw" form. Week after week, they patiently waded through early and evolving rough drafts. They'd sometimes be kept waiting as I made copies of a chapter I had just finished and then ran over to study and process it with them. Their prayers, honesty, feedback, encouragement, and support was invaluable and is reflected throughout the pages of this book. I love and appreciate you all more than I can say.

Healing isn't a formula. It's a journey.

Healing comes in layers. It's a process, but **not** a formula. We each have unique wounds that require unique Treatment. The books below chronicle the lessons, truths, and comfort I received on my ongoing healing journey. God gently showed me, led me, and continues to lead me through the process of **Acknowledge**, **Unravel**, And **Rewire**. Experiencing His intense, personal, and tender love through this process has made all the difference.

I pray you find the process and principles the Healer taught me helpful as you walk out your own individualized healing path.

Acknowledge your invisible wounds.

Unravel the roots of your pain.

Rewire your heart and mind.

Available on Amazon:
Invisible Wounds: *Hope While You're Hurting*
Unraveled Roots: *Exposing the Hidden Causes of Damaging Behaviors*
Rewired Heart: *Finding the Freedom of a Whole New You*

notes

1 Charles Spurgeon, from "Christ's Hospital" (1890), *Metropolitan Tabernacle Pulpit, vol. 38*, sermon 2260 (Edinburgh, United Kingdom: Banner of Truth, 1987).

2 Charles Spurgeon, from "The Common Salvation," *Metropolitan Tabernacle Pulpit, vol. 41*, sermon 2412 (Pasadena: Pilgrim Publications, 1975).

3 Taken from *The New Strong's Exhaustive Concordance of the Bible* by James Strong, LL.D, S.T.D. Copyright © 1990 by James Strong, LL.D, S.T.D. Used by permission of Thomas Nelson. www.thomasnelson.com

4 Henry Drummond, *The Greatest Thing In the World and Other Addresses* (United States, Merchant Books, 2009), 39.

Made in the USA
Las Vegas, NV
28 January 2021